Alice Taylor

I grew up on a farm in north Cork overlooking the Kerry mountains. At the time, rural houses like ours had neither electricity nor piped water, so life for women was not easy. Every day of the year I witnessed the amazing coping ability and resourcefulness of the women in my community. Of necessity, they bonded together to sustain their families and mastered the art of making do, while also developing their creativity. I grew up feeling that through their connectedness to each other, and to the land and animals, they nurtured the soul of Ireland. In today's world their daughters and granddaughters live and work in communities all around the country, continuing to keep the lifeblood pulsing through the veins of Irish life, especially through their voluntary work. They are the unheralded and unsung heroes of our past and present.

ALICE TAYLOR'S RECENT BOOKS:

Do You Remember?

And Time Stood Still

The Gift of a Garden

To School through the Fields

(special edition)

For a complete list, see www.obrien.ie

The Women

ABOUT *DO YOU REMEMBER?*

'A thoroughly enjoyable read.' ***Irish Country Magazine***

'A journey into nostalgia with spiritual overtones.'

Irish Independent

'Abounds in anecdotes of Irish rural life in former times, told in Alice's Taylor's distinctive, homely style.'

The Opinion

ABOUT *THE GIFT OF A GARDEN*

'Illuminated by the glowing photographs of Emma Byrne, enriched by such stories as the tree-planting *meitheal*, the gathering of manure and the history of the garden shed, *The Gift of a Garden* is itself a gift.'

Irish Examiner

'Alice is a storyteller writing about the plants and the people she loves, making this a delightful read.'

Country Gardener Magazine

ABOUT *AND TIME STOOD STILL*

'*And Time Stood Still* warmed my heart and reminded me of the value of family, friendship and community.'

Irish Independent

'Anybody who has lost someone can find solace in this book.' ***Arena*, RTÉ Radio 1**

The Women

Alice Taylor

photographs by Emma Byrne

BRANDON

First published 2015 by Brandon,
an imprint of The O'Brien Press Ltd,
12 Terenure Road East, Rathgar,
Dublin 6, Ireland
D06 HD27
Tel: +353 1 4923333; Fax: +353 1 4922777
E-mail: books@obrien.ie.
Website: www.obrien.ie

ISBN: 978-1-84717-788-9

10 9 8 7 6 5 4 3 2 1
22 21 20 19 18 17 16 15

Printed and bound in Poland by Białostockie Zakłady
Graficzne S.A.
The paper in this book is produced using pulp from
managed forests.

Dedication

To Eileen of Farnagow,
who enriches all our lives

Contents

Introduction

Sometimes in life you hit a wall. You are down to the wire. You need the motivation to begin again, just a little spark of inspiration and stimulation. Then you meet someone who ignites that spark. It lights the way forward and suddenly you can see where you are going. For me this special spark glows from the lives of inspirational women. – women who move with tranquility and purpose through their lives, opening up possibilities around them. They quietly reach out to others and leave behind imprints of comfort and encouragement.

My inspirational women are not well-known women. They live seemingly ordinary lives but they enrich the society in which we live. They swim beneath the tide of life and quietly change the currents of their time. They are the glue that holds society together. These women are the biblical stone rejected by the builder that became the cornerstone. They were and still are the silent cornerstones of our world.

The lives of these women are an untold story. Some still live among us and others are long gone – extraordinary women who because they were and are perceived to be ordinary never had their story told. We Irish walk in the footprints of great women. Women who lived through hard times on farms, in villages, towns and cities. They are often invisible in our history books – only a tiny handful are written about or celebrated.

The women I want to celebrate are often farm women who wrested a living from the land and raised large families on very limited resources. These are the women of my childhood years, who lived all around us on our hillfarm in north Cork. The term 'working wives' had yet to be coined, but it could certainly be used to describe them – they were the original working wives. Their workplace was the farmyard, but because it was adjacent to their home they were perceived as stay-at-home wives. But proximity to the job did not lighten their workload, which could be hard and demanding. They were the multitaskers of their time and added substantially to family incomes.

It is sobering to remember that the grandmothers of today's grandmothers were the first generation after the Great Famine. Those grandmothers were born into an Ireland still reeling from the hunger pangs of famine. Their habits were formed at a time of huge poverty and starvation. How did they move on to live with such grace and generosity, I wonder? Because that's what I saw in them – they were caring, generous women. And they passed this on to their daughters and granddaughters.

For our grandmothers the worst aspect of life was the almost guaranteed loss of their young adult children to emigration. I don't know how their hearts didn't break, and stay broken. Emigration for them and for generations to come was a necessary evil that wrenched children from families, children whom these mothers might never see again, children who faced huge risks in faraway places.

Their last farewell gathering earned the term 'The American Wake', and it was, to all intents and purposes, a wake, because even though there was no death, there was still the sense of a final parting. Some emigrants never again came back. Some felt that the fare home would cost too much, so they sent the money back instead to help out back home. Others got immersed in their new way of life and severed all connections with home, and some fell through the cracks of a new, challenging world and were never heard from again. The mothers they left behind had to dry their tears and turn their faces to the job of survival. I can only imagine the sadness and emptiness of this. And the courage needed to face life without the children.

The voyage to America took months, though with time that journey gradually dwindled to six weeks. The first letter from America, known as the 'landing letter' and telling of the emigrant's arrival, often took months to come back home. But how could any letter describe the tough challenges that these young people faced in a strange country and the hard lump of homesickness they endured? Most of the emigrants were very aware of the home situation and usually painted happy pictures of a new life to avoid worrying already burdened parents. Brian Friel depicted it on stage in *The Loves of Cass McGuire*.

Slowly, American and English money leaked back and eased the burden of poverty at home and also often paved the way for other American wakes when siblings joined the early departures in their new country. The foreign money did work wonders. It kept food on the table, bought extra fields to make farms viable, re-roofed houses, put cattle on the land and clothed younger siblings. The emigrants were still part of the home. American dollars and English pounds kept the home fires burning.

Other young women left home in a different way. Young idealistic girls went into the many convents dotted around the country. Coming out of homes burning with the religious fervour of the time, they dreamt of bringing some of this zeal to foreign lands. Other nuns stayed at home to educate our young and run our hospitals, and some joined contemplative orders and are still providing pools of peace in a frazzled world.

Out in the fields the farm women saved the hay, cut the corn and drew turf from the bog. Their town and city sisters reared large families on meagre wages, often supplemented by cleaning other people's homes and offices. The tenements where they lived are now replaced by high-rise apartments.

This book is a salutation to all those women, those who stayed at home and those who emigrated. They kept a light glowing in the windows, and they kept the doors open in the homes of Ireland. Some of these doors and windows are long gone and the ruins of old thatched cottages and stone farmhouses are buried in remote corners of our landscape. But great women who drew water from the well and lived close to the earth once inhabited those houses. Every spring on Rogation Day they went out with holy water to bless the crops, as their Celtic ancestors had done before them.

Despite swimming against the tide of poverty and despite their lack of inheritance rights, our female ancestors left us a rich heritage. So let us remember and celebrate them with appreciation and respect.

Chapter 1

The Candle Lighter: the Mother

Whenever we were faced with a formidable undertaking on the home farm my mother would say, 'Isn't it great that we have the mind on us to do it.' And if we questioned our ability to succeed, her answer invariably was, 'Why wouldn't we?' She firmly believed that you could do anything if you thought you could do it, and once you got going nothing could stop you. Getting going was to her what it was all about. Her 'can do' attitude, I'm convinced, was forged from the hard practical challenges facing women in their everyday lives at that time, with no electricity, no running water, no modern machines to help with the tough jobs. This must have made these women strong, both physically and mentally.

But there was a softness and warmth in my mother as well. Whenever any of her children or neighbours was facing a challenge she would light a candle and place it in a glass bowl at the centre of the parlour table. It was her way of reminding God to keep an eye on things. If she judged that the candle needed backup, she would kneel by the table silently saying the rosary. In later years she was often contacted by children and grandchildren from all over the world pleading with her to light her candle, and they knew it would be accompanied by her prayers. It was heart-warming to imagine her loving support back in the home place. At times of tumult I now light the candle. Mothers create the inner essence of their daughters.

In 1928 my mother moved from her family farm in north Cork to my father's farm a few miles over the road where she grafted onto a new family tree. She had moved into a mortgage-free house and a job for life. As was the custom of the time, I assume that she brought a 'fortune' with her. Daughters like my mother, who worked in the home place, did not get a wage as such, but when they married they were given a lump sum, a kind of dowry. That fortune was then invested in the farm or perhaps was given to a sister-in-law to enable her to move on to another farm. It was said that the same fortune moved from farm to farm all around Munster!

As a child, my mother walked the three miles to and from the local national school in the nearest town every day. At that time, during the War of Independence, the Black and Tan soldiers were everywhere. They were unpredictable, untrained soldiers with a reputation for savagery and lawlessness. The children would hide in a ditch when they heard the Tan lorries coming – one time the soldiers had pointed their guns at them and fired bullets over their heads, and after that the youngsters disappeared off the road instantly at the sound of those engines.

She had one brother and one sister, but she married into a much larger family, as my father had two sisters and six brothers. His parents were both dead, so she did not have a mother-in-law or father-in-law, but the youngest brother and sister were still living on the farm when she came there. But sharing her home with in-laws was no hardship to my mother as she had come from a home where many members of the extended family came and went over the years.

She often told us about her first social challenge in her new home, which was to host the wedding breakfast of her new sister-in-law. The reception was to be held in the home place, with a magnificent wedding cake that the bride-to-be had made taking pride of place in the centre of the parlour table. Older brothers with wives and children came back for their sister's wedding and while the ceremony was taking place at the church all the children were left to play in the garden. One curious young lad spotted the beautiful cake through the parlour window. He was mesmerised and called the others to view it. They had never seen anything quite like this cake. The temptation proved too great and in they went, and the young lad merrily dished out slices of cake to his assembled cousins.

When the wedding party returned, the bride was not impressed! It wasn't a great start to my mother's career as hostess in her new home. My father and mother tried to calm troubled waters but it was a long time before that particular brother was allowed by his sister to forget the misdemeanours of his son. But in later years she had indeed forgotten all about it. She had married a man who had an extensive orchard and every autumn when we were children she visited bearing gifts of huge bags of apples; the cake and the erring boy were never mentioned.

My mother was of the belief that when you married your husband, you also married his family. Once in later years, when I was airing my views about the disadvantages of having my husband's aunt living next door, she promptly told me that when you denigrated your husband's family you denigrated your husband. That put a stop to my pontificating! But she was not blind to the family flaws of her own new family tree. She informed me, in an amused tone of voice, that early in marriage she had discovered that the Taylors thought they knew better than everybody else. I never forgot that little bit of wisdom. As a Taylor, it's a trait with which I constantly struggle.

It was to my mother's advantage that she was not into constantly airing her views but moved with quiet determination among her more loquacious in-laws. But she had firmly held convictions about the importance of family, home life and the need to keep everybody in the house well fed and nourished. Sometimes my father went on a rant about household expenses, declaring that there was enough waste in our house to rear a whole other family. There were permanent callers to the house as neighbours moved freely between each other's homes and my mother kept an open-door policy. All had to be fed or at least offered some form of hospitality. Then too, the 'Travelling People', known at the time as 'Tinkers', as the menfolk were tinsmiths, called regularly and never left empty-handed. If my father was on one of his economy drives he would tell my mother that they were all better fed than us – to which my mother simply turned a deaf ear and continued blithely on her way. She regarded the kitchen table as her domain.

The main source of food at the time was the pig. This too was women's business, apart from the actual slaughtering which was carried out by our Uncle Daniel, who was known for the skill. Dealing with the dead pig was a communal affair. Neighbouring women came together to fill the sausages and puddings and each had a different recipe, but the recipe of the woman of the house prevailed at her pudding filling. We all enjoyed savouring the different flavours throughout the year. Filling the puddings, as it was called, took over the whole house, with disgusting-looking buckets of pig's guts standing all around the kitchen, as well as enamel buckets full of boiled blood laced with herbs and all kinds of mysterious concoctions. There was a black-pudding mix and a white-pudding mix. It was a messy business, but finally the mixture was pushed into a mincer to which a funnel was attached, and over this went the pig's well-washed gut, which was then filled with the mixture. It came out in long, thick tubes, and my mother cut it at intervals into loops, then plunged them into a pot of boiling water that stood on the open fire. Then she filed them along the handle of a brush until they cooled. Nowadays we can buy the world-famous Clonakilty black pudding in most supermarkets, but it all began with the resourceful women in the farmhouses of rural Ireland. Preserving every bit of food the pig supplied was most important. Fresh porksteaks as well as the home-filled sausages and puddings were distributed among the neighbours, who returned the compliment when their pig was slaughtered. Thus fresh meat was had more often throughout the community.

After the pudding-making, the men gathered to salt the pig. Then my mother took over again to fill the pickle barrel in which the meat was preserved. This was done very carefully as it would feed her household throughout the year. It was a very precise process. She layered the bottom of the scrubbed-out and well-scalded tall timber barrel with a layer of salt. As each layer of salted bacon went in, more salt was laid between the layers until the barrel was full of meat. She drew buckets of spring water from the well in the field behind the house to pour into the barrel over the meat. But first more salt was added to the water, and in order to ascertain that there was sufficient salt in the water she placed an egg on top – if the egg floated, there was enough salt, but if it sank, more had to be added. When she had the barrel filled with pickle and bacon she placed a large well-washed stone or a heavy plank of wood on top of the meat to prevent floating. Later she lifted the bacon out of the barrel and hung it off hooks along the kitchen ceiling where it cured slowly. She took particular care of the ham and to this day I struggle to achieve the flavour of her wonderful Christmas ham.

She had seven children, the youngest of whom died when he was four, which caused her immense grief. In later years when we talked about it, she told me quietly, 'I should not have mourned Connie so deeply or for so long.' 'But, Mom,' I protested, 'he was only four and it was heart-breaking.' 'I know that,' she said, 'but I got bogged down in my own grief and forgot about the effect it was having on your father and the rest of you.' She felt that women had to be constantly strong and comforting for the sake of the whole family; they set the tone. That conversation with my mother has always stayed with me.

She was a woman of quiet ways and deep wisdom. She never boasted about our achievements but enjoyed whatever little triumphs we had quietly in her own heart. I recall one time when a woman who was forever boasting about her wonderfully talented family left our house after a long, boring visit, my mother rose from her chair, saying in a puzzled voice, 'One would wonder what was all that telling about!' My mother believed that the facts should be allowed to speak for themselves.

The workload of our mothers and grandmothers was unbelievable. As well as rearing large families in houses that had no electricity, no piped water and no labour-saving devices, they milked cows and fed calves, pigs, hens, ducks and geese every day of the year. They managed the larger animals too, looked after their housing and nursed them when they were sick or giving birth – apart from the cows, which was usually, though not always, a man's job.

By the time the younger children got up in the morning at around seven o'clock, my mother was already out with my father and older brother and sisters milking the cows. It was the job of another sister to call us and then light the fire and lay the table for breakfast. A large pot of porridge was always by the fire; my mother made it the previous night and left it to cook slowly on the warm cinders. She was a staunch believer in a good breakfast, maintaining that it saw you through the day, so after the porridge came boiled eggs and her own homemade brown bread. We then prepared our own lunches and as we were leaving the house my mother was usually on her way in. My sisters had come in earlier from milking to get ready for school.

After breakfast my father took the milk to the creamery and my mother started what were known as her 'outside jobs'. First on the agenda was feeding the now-bawling calves. They were definitely the loudest of all the animals, but every other animal around the yard was also yelling in hungry protest! The baby calves were bucket-fed individually and the larger ones herded around a trough into which my mother poured buckets of milk. The slugged it all back very rapidly. Then they were all released out into the fields where they danced with delighted freedom. Next on the feeding list were the pigs, and this was a tough job. Their feed had first to be mixed in a large timber tub in the mess house, then my mother faced the onslaught of the demanding pigs when she opened their door – and tried to maintain her balance as she struggled over to their circular iron trough in the middle of the piggery. They always strove to upend the bucket, but once its contents made it into the trough they buried their snouts and silence reigned. Then the timid hens got their rations, and when released from the confines of the henhouse they shrilled with delight and ran around my mother, pecking up the scattered oats. They were joined by flocks of waiting birds who swooped down from the surrounding trees. Then the geese and ducks were released and they headed off down the fields towards the river. Gradually all the animals were fed and quietened.

On her way back into the kitchen again my mother picked up a bucket of turf and an armful of blocks of wood to stoke up the fire, which by this time was beginning to run out of steam. Then it was time to tidy the kitchen, wash up the breakfast ware and do the baking. Every day she baked one large cake of brown bread and one white. While the bread was baking, she prepared the dinner – we were the ordinary people that Jackie Healy Rae referred to as having their dinner in the middle of the day. Sometimes, if it was not already done, my mother went to a field near the house and dug up the potatoes and cut the cabbage and turnips that were our staple diet. If the spring-water supply was running low, she went to the well for a bucket of water. This water was brought into the kitchen in a white enamel bucket which stood on a side table and was strictly for drinking and making tea. Nobody would dream of putting it to any other use. Beside our house there was a constant supply of other water that ran down from the hill further up the farm, and in our yard it ran into a pipe that we called 'the spout', and under this spout we washed the potatoes and anything else requiring a good scrub. Once she had washed the potatoes under the spout she put everything in pots over the open fire to cook. While the dinner was cooking she went upstairs to make the beds. Then when all the pots were deemed ready, she laid the table, took down the whistle off its hook and went to the door to summon the hungry in from the fields. Anyone helping on the farm was included in the head count and dinner was put aside for the schoolchildren. If it was hay-making or harvest time the dinners had to be multiplied to match the size of the *meitheal*. Despite all the preparation involved, my mother always maintained that feeding people presented no problem once the supplies were sufficient, and she believed that a 'good table', as she termed it, was an important part of any home.

When she had unexpected visitors she was always delighted to be able to make them welcome with a nice meal. As we lived at the end of a long boreen about three miles from the nearest town, with no corner shop nearby to provide a back-up in this situation, this was not always easy. But she had the ability to whip up something nice with very few reserves and was a great believer in the presentation power of fine china on a good tablecloth.

If it was a Monday the family wash, which was a marathon of soaking, washing, lathering, scrubbing on the board, rinsing, boiling and hanging out to dry had to be packed somehow into this busy schedule. The annual quilt- and blanket-washing could spread over a few days and would turn the kitchen into a temporary lake. The decision to wash blankets depended totally on the weather and the highest recommendation that my mother could give to a day was to say that it was ideal for washing blankets. In her opinion, days came no better than that.

After dinner she brought down the sewing machine from the parlour and put it on the kitchen table. She sewed and patched our clothes and often it was then that neighbouring women from across the fields would arrive for a chat. My mother loved good-quality material and put a lot of consideration into the purchase of good wool blankets and pure cotton sheets, and if her budget did not stretch to quality cotton she made the sheets herself from the white bags in which the flour came home from the mill. These bags were made of either rough linen or good quality cotton, and when washed and bleached could be turned into long-lasting sheets, pillow cases and aprons. She gathered these throughout the year and those she did not get around to using were put into Aunt Kate's trunk to await her visit – Aunt Kate was our amazing family seamstress.

Some time in her day she went out and gathered the eggs from the outhouses around the farmyard. The hens had their own house with built-in laying boxes, but they often preferred to make their nests in the barn and the horses' mangers. Needless to mention, the horses would be delighted to come home after a hard day's work out in the fields and polish off a nestful of eggs to put a gloss on their coats. We also had a greyhound who was partial to a raw egg tonic and she had to be tied up every day until my mother had gathered the eggs.

Then it was time for the customary four o'clock tea. After that came the time for 'stray jobs', as she used to say. If it was fruit-picking season, she cracked into jam-making action. Other jobs might include making a bran mix for a newly calved cow or tending to a calf who had the scour. The scour, which was a bad dose of diarrhoea, was the scourge of the baby calf world and had to be controlled as it was highly infectious. After that it was time to feed the calves, pigs and hens again and house them all down for the night. At around six o'clock the cows were brought home for milking and when that was over, the yard work was finished for the day. In the summer the cows were turned out into the fields for the night, and then it was supper time.

After supper came darning time and she sat beneath the oil lamp surrounded by knitted jumpers and socks that had numerous holes. As she darned we did our lessons, and she chatted with neighbouring men who often gathered around the fire in evening time. Her last job of the night was to make the porridge and to arrange the brought-in washing on the backs of chairs around the fire to make sure that the clothes were well aired.

Despite her incredible workload I have no memory of my mother being in a hurry. She always had the time to sit down and talk to us and to the neighbours. Sometimes in the summer evenings she went back into the old fort behind our house where my father had planted trees and she gathered bundles of sticks for the fire, and sometimes took a metal gallon-sized can to collect blackberries for jam-making. Then too, she might go for a long walk up through the fields and she'd be gone for hours. This, I think, was her quiet, meditative time when she regained her equilibrium out in the silence of the fields and came home at peace with her world. My father would occasionally say to her, 'Lena, when you disappear up into the glen would you take a whistle with you because if you fall down into a hole up there we'll never find you?' To this request she turned a deaf ear. Turning a deaf ear was her strategy when the necessity arose.

As a child I took all her hard work for granted, but now in hindsight I wonder how she found the time to do all that had to be done and yet have time to go across the fields to neighbours who were ill or needed help. Every journey in those days took a lot of time. Every week she went back the road to visit her own mother and each Sunday when going to Mass she took a cake of brown bread and bottles of milk to an old neighbour in town. I think that she somehow never heard of hurry. One of her great blessings was that she never lost her head in a crisis – that was my father's speciality! But she calmed troubled waters around him and had the incredible skill of bringing things into perspective with a well-phrased placatory comment. When he was on a rampage about something that he deemed to be a disaster she'd remind him mildly, 'At least there is no one dead.' I sometimes recall that comment when I get my knickers in a knot over something that is annoying but will soon pass.

She was also a great radio listener and her day was punctuated by radio programmes. Normally a fan of Raidió Éireann, she turned over to the BBC for *Woman's Hour* and *Mrs Dale's Diary*. At night there were often arguments between my parents – and in later years, us children – as to what programme should be turned on, but during the day she had free choice. Much more traditional than my father, she came from a strong republican household, supporting Fianna Fáil and De Valera, whereas my father held totally different views and firmly believed that De Valera had ruined the finances of the country with his economic war. But they agreed to differ on politics and we joked that on polling day they should just stay at home as they cancelled each other out at the polls. And whereas my father held a slightly cynical view of some of the religious practices of the time, my mother was an unquestioning practitioner. Every night, without fail, we all went on our knees for the family rosary and she furnished each one of us with miraculous

CONGREGATION OF THE CHILDREN OF MARY
LENA TAYLOR
8 - 12 - 31

Chapter 2

This Land Was Her Land: Nana

The late John Moriarty, Kerry poet, philosopher and prophet of our time, wrote about taking care with his very young niece of a cow calving on the home farm. In the process the little girl told him that she too had come from her mother's tummy. When he asked her where her mother came from she told him from Nana's tummy, and when he asked where Nana had come from the little girl looked shocked at his lack of knowledge and unhesitatingly told him, 'Nana was always there.' It said a lot about the woman in question. The child perceived her Nana as the back wall of her world. John Moriarty's writings about his mother reveal an extraordinary person, a strong earthy woman who laid down a deep well of spirituality in her offspring.

Women like John Moriarty's mother were toughened by the hard work on the land and yet something in their deep being connected with the creativity of nature and the battle against the elements. The land was their master, their salvation, their nourishment and their constant challenge. In summer, when all was well, it was the face of God, but in winter, when they fought with its harshness, it was a battle with the Devil. But these women took it on and sometimes understood better than their men the nature of the land and the animals that survived on it.

John Moriarty's writings ring memory bells of my own grandmother. These women were forged from strong metal that enabled them to wrest a livelihood from the land. In England and maybe in Irish urban areas these grandmothers were usually called 'Granny', but in rural Ireland it was always 'Nana'.

In our family we called our grandmother Nana Ballyduane. I am not sure why we did not simply call her Nana, as she was the only one we had – our paternal grandmother was dead before any of us were born – but for some reason our maternal grandmother took her title from the townland in which she lived. It was almost as if she owned that whole townland, and in truth she often acted as if she did. When in later years my siblings and I talked about her I sometimes felt that we were each talking about a different person – there is no doubt that memory paints many pictures – but the general consensus, despite our varying recollections, was of a woman with whom you did not trifle. Widowed at a young age, she took over the running of the farm with efficient determination. My grandfather had been a gentle quiet man, with a sensitive diplomatic nature, so they were a good combination. He was often away as he traded in cattle, so Nana was well used to running the show on her own.

Many years later, at the very mention of his name her whole demeanour changed and she would smile in loving remembrance. I sensed that these two very different people had walked in harmony and, though he was gone, the face of her remembrance brought him back – and I felt that any man who could transform my grandmother so profoundly, even years after his death, had to be someone special.

When she came to live in Ballyduane, there was a mother-in-law, a father-in-law and a brother-in-law already in the house. It was not a large house, but a long, low thatched farmhouse common in the countryside at the time. Because she was no shrinking violet, it's difficult for me to imagine life in that house without a certain amount of conflict. But her in-laws have always remembered her as the woman who fitted in very well with them and contributed greatly to family harmony. Maybe the reason the family all got on together was because they were so busy trying to eke out a living off the land there was little time for bickering. Nana was a formidable six foot tall and her new mother-in-law was small in stature – and she was most impatient! Nana would sometimes recall that they would go out together in the mornings to bring home the cows for milking; some animals did not rise fast enough for her tiny mother-in-law so she would simply leap over them and continue to round up the fast movers, leaving the dawdlers to her daughter-in-law.

Nana was past the fresh flush of youth when she decided to enter the matrimonial field so she only had three children, which in today's world would be considered ample but at the time was considered a very small family. My mother was the eldest and took after her father, for which I was forever grateful! A few years after my grandmother's arrival in Ballyduane a sister-in-law died leaving a young son, and Nana Ballyduane brought this young lad home and reared him as her own. Various members of the family always felt free to come and stay, and a distant relation who came to help on the farm stayed for years.

It was wartime when Nana was a young married woman and the women of her generation played a huge part in the struggle for independence. She was a staunch republican and when the Black and Tans were raiding houses for young fellows who were waging guerrilla warfare and on the run, her home was on their list – these houses where the men would find shelter were known as 'safe houses'. It was a dangerous time, but she would not back down when the Tans raided. Sometimes the locals knew that the Tans were around and the lads would move on, but occasionally houses could be taken unawares. One night my grandmother had a nephew of her husband's hiding in the house and in the small hours of the morning the Tan lorries drove into the yard. The punishment for hiding a rebel could be pretty drastic – you might be burnt out or roughed up, or maybe worse – so she delayed opening up as long as possible to give him a chance to do whatever he could to render himself invisible. Finally, when the banging could no longer be withstood, she opened the door and the soldiers, in their hated black and tan uniforms, strode in and ransacked the house. She stood and watched, waiting for the young fellow to be discovered, but to her amazement it did not happen. As the Tans were leaving, the officer in charge, who had raided the house several times before, eyed her and said, 'You remind me of my mother.' 'Indeed!' she snapped back acidly. 'Your mother mustn't be up to much to rear a scoundrel like you.'

When they were gone, nobody moved for a long time because they had learned from experience that the Tans would sometimes double back and catch people unawares. Eventually judging it safe, she stood in the middle of the kitchen and called out, 'Where in the name of God are you?' Beside the fire was a long old wooden settle bed. This could open out into a bed but when closed up it looked just like a seat. Beneath the seat, however, was a space and in here bags of flour and sugar were usually stored. Nestled down amongst the bags was the young lad, who had watched the whole scene through a slit in the laths. The Tans had probably never seen a settle so had no idea of its hidden potential.

Accidents were always part of farming life and it usually fell to the woman of the house to deal with them. Nana never lost her head when there was a catastrophe but dealt with it calmly and efficiently. She had no medical training but had an innate sense of what to do, and once when one of the farm workers sustained a very serious injury and she rendered first aid until the doctor arrived, he told her that her prompt intervention had saved the young lad's life.

When her husband died she had the expertise and foresight to hire great workmen, whom she treated with the height of respect. Johnny came to her as a young lad and she trained him up to be a good farmer. But she did many of the 'man's' jobs herself too. The skill of killing a pig was usually a man's job, but she had mastered it. This barbaric exercise had to be executed with absolute precision to avoid undue suffering. She later taught Johnny how to do it. It was simply a job that *had* to be done and as there was no one else to do it she did not shrink from the undertaking; in fact, she did not shirk any tough job that had to be done. One time she evicted the local vet from her yard when she deemed that he was doing a bad job in assisting a cow who was having difficulty calving, and she took over the job herself, saving both mother and calf. In the world of male-dominated farming she never underestimated her own ability.

She kept track of all the animals on her farm and when preparing them for the fair she worked out exactly how much each was likely to fetch. Women did not attend the fairs as this was a men-only arena, but from her home base she controlled how things went, instructing Johnny on which tricky neighbours to avoid and which jobbers – cattle traders – were not to be trusted. Johnny knew exactly what the animal was expected to fetch and usually brought home the required amount. Her male neighbours knew that she was a force to be reckoned with and understood that just because she was a woman she was no pushover. She was very proud of the high productivity of her cows and kept a careful eye on her creamery returns. The creamery was also a male-dominated world from which she was excluded, but again from a distance she kept a wary eye on activities.

Amazingly for such an independent woman, at the age of seventy she decided that she had done enough work and took to her chair by the fire, from where she supervised the comings and goings of the household and farm. A saintly girl called Mary came to help her with the kitchen and yard work. Sometimes I was dispatched back to stay with Nana Ballyduane and Mary was the guardian who protected me from my grandmother's ire. Nana firmly believed that children should unquestioningly do exactly as they were instructed and if your performance was not up to her specifications she had an often-repeated reprimand: 'What does a badly done job say? It says do me all over again!' She did not countenance sitting down reading a book or gazing out the window at the sky when there was work to be done, and she often told me, 'There is nothing got from idleness only dirt and long nails.' The result was that I hid my books in the hay-barn and disappeared up there as often as possible. One time I was reading *A Tale of Two Cities* and felt that Nana would have fitted in very well in the period of the French Revolution and would have had no problem in whipping the head off a frilled, perfumed aristocrat whom she felt had wronged her of her livelihood and stolen her lands!

But sometimes, late in the evening, she thawed out and lapsed into remembrances as she sat by the fire, and then it was lovely to sit and listen. Years afterwards I regretted not having paid enough attention, as she had amazing recall. She told of taking butter from her childhood home in Cullen up along the old 'butter road' to the Cork market, where there was a worldwide trade in butter at the time. Those were tough times and it was a constant struggle to keep food on the table.

Occasionally during her later years she would decide that it was finally time to bow out, and she would summon the priest and doctor to verify her decision. If their diagnoses were different to hers she would be extremely annoyed but would decide to rise from her bed and resume life for another while. When she had one of these 'figarioes' as my father called them, my uncle would come for my mother and inform us, 'Herself has a touch of Oliver.' I have no idea what that expression meant, but it entered our family lore and if you were having a fit of the blues it was always termed 'a touch of Oliver'.

She had an insatiable thirst for political news and the daily copy of the *Irish Press* was her bible, but if it was sold out my uncle brought the local *Cork Examiner*, which she contemptuously referred to as 'Crosby's Blue Rag', after the proprietor, and she shoved it under the kettle on the fire! She and my father had totally conflicting political views, so for the sake of family harmony they never discussed politics. I think my father felt at a disadvantage anyway, as, due to her age and the fact that she was his mother-in-law, they were not on a level playing field.

When I was staying with her I always shared her bed, which was a high black iron bed with big brass knobs top and bottom. Over the wire springs at the base was a horse-hair mattress and on that was a deep feather tick, covered by strong cotton sheets, and then layers of wool blankets; the whole thing was topped with a patchwork quilt and a mountain of feather pillows on which to rest our heads. To get into it I had to hoist myself up with the help of the bottom bedpost and then scramble up along the quilt and burrow down under the blankets. I was always in bed before she began her bedtime ritual and undressing ceremony.

The only light came from the candle in the sconce on the deep narrow window, through which she peered out at the night sky to forecast the following day's weather. Then she did a monologue on the state of the farm fields stretching out in front of her. She loved the land and in her nightly survey described the state of each field. The Clune Field was her favourite and the name rolled off her tongue like softly whipped cream. Beside it the Well Field stretched down the side of an adjoining hill and always had a great grass crop; in a shaded corner a deep well provided a non-stop supply of sparkling clear water. Up to the left was Andy's Field, which got its name from a man of a previous generation who had lived there. In her nightly homily she blessed all her fields. That done, she went to the weights-and-chains clock beside the large fireplace and by some complicated manoeuvring she managed to draw down one chain, which drew up the other one that bore a heavy pendulum. This exercise, known simply as 'winding the clock', ensured that it kept going and pealed out musically on the hour and half-hour. Then she was ready for her undressing ritual.

One of my strongest memories of her is of her clothing. Women of her age wore a great array of clothes in multiple layers. The ritual of her undressing when going to bed had to be seen to be believed. As a child I found it fascinating. First off was her black bonnet, which was hung off the bottom bedpost, followed by the black crochet cape from around her shoulders, and this was placed carefully over the back of the high chair beside the bed. Then she returned to the window to view the fields one more time and began to ease open the long row of small covered buttons down the front of her black velvet blouse. As she did this she sometimes left the window view and rambled around the room from where she regaled me with stories of long-gone ancestors whose portraits still hung on the walls or were arrayed along the marble mantelpiece. The buttons undone, the blouse joined the cape on the back of the chair. With the removal of the blouse, rows of underwear, with their lower half disappearing beneath her long black skirt, came into view. Some pieces of underwear had long sleeves and others short, and they were laced up the front. She undid the large button at the back of her long black skirt, and it slid downwards in a black crumpled heap around her ankles. This revealed a bright red gathered petticoat and I always regretted that this beautiful daring garment was hidden by the dull black skirt. When I voiced this opinion once I was simply told to hush up. She stepped out of the skirt and it was laid carefully across the seat of the chair. The petticoat followed the skirt onto the chair and long pink bloomers that stretched from her waist down to her knees made their appearance. She eased up

30•9•76
FIVE POUNDS
FIVE POUNDS

if sniffing is good for the muscles, I benefited as well. Next she went to a deep narrow press behind the trailing chains of the clock, prised it open with a tiny key and removed a small blue bottle full of a most obnoxious-smelling liquid called Cascara, a kind of natural laxative made from tree bark. She carefully poured out a measure into a small glass that had marks etched up along the side. Then she slowly savoured it as if it were rare Midleton whiskey. After that she got her bottle of holy water and doused the room, including me in the shower.

All done, she boarded the bed. Her bodily requirements had been seen to and now it was time for her spirit, and so began the Rosary and a long list of prayers. By then sleep was beginning to get the better of me, and when my mumbled Holy Marys trailed to a standstill I would get a poke in the ribs to stimulate wakefulness. But she finally gave up and I drifted off to sleep as invocations for heavenly blessings circulated around the bed.

Chapter 3

A Great Pair of Hands

When Aunt Kate came to stay she took over the parlour and turned it into an Aladdin's cave. The large table at the centre disappeared under a mountain of material for the multiplicity of creative transformations that were about to take place. Aunt Kate could sew, knit, embroider, crochet, make lace, quilt and do patchwork. While many of the neighbours were skilled in some of these accomplishments, Aunt Kate had mastered them all, and my grandmother used to say that she was blessed with a great pair of hands and a brain to match. The morning after her arrival, down from the black loft came Aunt Kate's trunk

The Singer Manufacturing Co.
SINGER

– in our old farmhouse the attic was graphically known as the 'black' loft because that is exactly what it was, with one tiny window dimly illuminating its dusty interior. Up there were the abandoned cradle, retired milk churns, half-made beehives, newspapers that my mother planned to read when more leisurely days came her way, and everything that she deemed might come in handy some day.

Hidden under the sloping roof was Aunt Kate's trunk, waiting to be dragged out of hibernation when she came to stay. She usually came twice a year, midsummer and midwinter. On her midsummer visit, the doors and windows of the parlour were thrown open and the aroma of the garden filtered in, and sometimes Aunt Kate took her chair outside and did hand-sewing under what we called Andy Connie's tree. Andy Connie was an uncle of my father, and when he came to stay he always claimed that all night this tree swayed in the breeze and sang 'Andy Connie, Andy Connie…'.

If she was under the Andy Connie tree when we came home from school she would patiently show us how to put up stitches on our small knitting needles and teach us how to do 'under, around and over' until we finally got the hang of it. If we lost a knitting needle she introduced us to the skill of creating one from the quill of a goose wing. Learning to knit at school had been a stress test, but Aunt Kate turned it into a labour of love.

On her winter visit the window and door of the parlour

were closed against cold and draughts. When the fire was lit the room was filled with the whiff of the burning logs and turf and of the great array of materials airing in the heat.

Getting Aunt Kate's trunk down from the black loft and into the parlour was not a job for the faint-hearted. Leading from the loft down into a room off the parlour there was a steep stairs, which had many missing steps that my father planned to replace one day, but in the meantime you had to have the agility of an acrobat to arrive safely at base. Manoeuvring the heavy trunk down this treacherous incline was paramount to mastering the challenges of a steep ski slope. If my father was involved, it was a miracle that the trunk did not go on fire, ignited by the flood of inflammatory language that accompanied its descent. The descent wasn't made easier by the fact that the trunk was made of wood, edged with brass, and was quite weighty in its own right. Then, throughout the year, lots of things had been thrown into it – sheets with see-through patches, threadbare blankets, all sorts of worn knits, dresses deemed too short, too small or too tight, and any item gone past its wear-by date. When my mother was in doubt about what to do with any abandoned garment, Aunt Kate's trunk solved the problem. Its cavernous depths swallowed all! So it was almost impossible to lift it and it had to be shunted along in stops and starts. However, with many thumps and bumps it would finally arrive at its destination.

Once the word went around that Aunt Kate was in residence the local women gathered like bees to a honey pot. Now was the time to go into their press under the stairs and rescue that abandoned piece of knitting that had proved too complicated. Aunt Kate would cast her experienced eye over a half-knit sock and with a quick flick of the needles and a swirl of the knitting wool would begin to turn the complicated heel or close the reluctant toe and gently guide the knitter back into action. She could knit all kinds of everything. Plain, purl, Fair Isle, cable all ran off her needles like a continuous waterfall. While doing the most complicated Fair Isle patterns, involving a stream of different-coloured wools pouring through her fingers, she could unconcernedly carry on the most interesting conversation or keep her eye on a meandering toddler. She had a stack of old knitting patterns and the local women checked them out and brought some of their own patterns to discuss the pitfalls, merits and possibilities involved in following them. This exchange of ideas and knitting patterns often turned into a tea party.

Most husbands and children at the time were togged out in hand-knit socks and jumpers, and knitting wool was sold in Denny Ben's draper's shop in town. Wool came in long hanks and had to be wound into balls for more convenient handling. Winding the thread, as it was known, involved two people, one with outstretched arms, like a supplicant in prayer, holding the hank from wrist to wrist so that the winder had easy access to the stretched-out wool while winding it into balls. This could lead to weary arm muscles if the holder did not have great muscular strength. Sometimes a protesting male, not otherwise occupied, could be hauled in to hold the hank. If no willing body was available, you had to make do with the backs of chairs and drape the hank across two of them. The *súgán* kitchen chairs with their upright ears were well suited to this job. Almost every household boasted a knitter and knitting tastes fluctuated between plain, Fair Isle and cable. Balls of leftover knitting wool were exchanged between the women to be used for darning, which was an ongoing necessity as toes, heels and elbows were constantly making undesirable public appearances.

Most clothes, especially the children's, were made at home and material was carefully chosen in Denny Ben's on a Sunday after Mass, when remnants were also picked up to patch and extend the life of many items of clothing. Nothing was thrown away and every piece of clothing had a reincarnation into another life after a temporary demise in Aunt Kate's trunk. Aunt Kate could merge two small dresses together and create one lovely dress. We never had any misgivings about her creations because they were always smart and flattering. At the time if your legs grew too long for your coat or dress and it was deemed too short, the solution was to add a piece along the bottom. Usually this looked exactly what it was, a tack-on job! But Aunt Kate had the skill to pick up a colour already dominant in the garment and make it appear like deliberate colour coordination. In contrast, my grandmother never achieved the same effect because she believed that all that mattered was serviceability and practicality. Her dressmaking creed was: 'Make it large enough and they will grow into it', which did not lend itself to well-fitted elegance, whereas Aunt Kate had a sense of style. My grandmother held Kate in the highest esteem and perceived her as having totally mastered what she termed 'the art of making do'. My grandmother's judgement of a bad housekeeper was that she could 'not even face a shirt', but Aunt Kate turned frayed shirt collars back to front to give them a longer life, and the good back of a shirt was often transferred to replace the battered front.

She also extended the life of sheets with see-through middles by cutting them up the centre and bringing the sides to the middle. This was termed 'turning the sheets'. A turned sheet would live to serve a few more years, though the seam down the centre had to be taken into consideration when positioning your lower regions at night. Throughout the year my mother collected large flour bags that came from the mill. These were made of good cotton and when well washed and boiled were turned to many uses. They became aprons, tea towels and pillow cases and when sewn together made sheets that were slightly abrasive and could also provide a stimulating skin massage! These bags were also used as a trim along the tops of blankets to prevent fraying.

Aunt Kate turned coats and jackets inside out, giving them a whole new look, and she perked up faded dresses with a smart new lace or crochet collar. She could crochet effortlessly, but lacemaking required more concentration as she stitched the fragile material delicately back and forth. Knitting and sewing came easily to most of the neighbouring women, but they were eager to master the art of crocheting and lacemaking with Kate. The delicate table centres and lace runners that she helped them create brought a touch of elegance to houses where frugality was, of necessity, the way of life. They stitched some of their lace and crochet pieces on to pillow cases and this gave their beds a well-dressed appearance when special visitors came to stay.

But the most challenging undertaking was quilting, which was a communal activity. The old quilting frame was brought down from the black loft and once this was opened out it had to be left *in situ* until the job was done as it was a difficult task to get the whole thing in place. First to go on the frame was a well-worn blanket or good heavy twill sheet that was to be the back of the quilt, which could later, if desired, be covered with another fabric. Sheep's wool was stitched onto this with good strong thread, using a good strong needle. Usually the No. 10 reel of thread was the man for this job. Thread at the time was not easily come by due to rationing, so No. 10 was used with great care. This was slow, exacting work, as you had to make sure that each piece of wool was firmly secured in place. When this was achieved, the wool was covered over with another sheet or a piece of fabric. Then came the skill of patchworking, when old dresses and shirts were cut into pieces and carefully colour coordinated before being sewn together. This was when the contents of Aunt Kate's trunk came into their own. The exercise resembled the making of a colourful jigsaw and Aunt Kate, who had a creative eye for colour coordination, quietly directed the whole operation. The pieces were stitched together by hand and then sewn onto the quilt. As the pieces were cut and sewn, stories were told about the different garments and the whole session turned into a storytelling saga interwoven with tea breaks. The entire undertaking could spread over weeks. When the quilt was complete, not only did it keep the family warm in the future but it also told the story of the family's past.

This type of quilt was very warm but not too heavy. However, Aunt Kate and the other women could also turn out much heavier and warmer quilts. For this, more substantial material than wool was used for the lining and heavier garments were cut up for the patchwork pieces. When completed, these quilts were indeed weighty creations. But on cold winter nights when Jack Frost drove his nose through non-double glazed windows and penetrated unheated homes, these gigantic quilts formed a protective barrier between the freezing cold and the slumbering residents, even though sometimes the sleeper might be hard put to achieve an effortless turnover beneath one. Washing these heavy quilts took place only at the height of summer because they had to be laid out on the grass or across hedges to dry as no clothesline was strong enough to bear the burden.

Making ticks for the beds was another one of Aunt Kate's undertakings. My mother bought ticking by the yard in Denny Ben's, where huge rolls of material were stacked on floor-to-ceiling shelving. This ticking was extremely strong navy and white fabric, and the Singer sewing machine was used to make the tick, which was the equivalent of our present-day duvet, except that instead of sleeping under the tick we slept on it. The Singer sewing machine was a resident in most homes. My mother inherited hers from my grandmother and often neighbours without a machine came across the fields to use it. When the tick, which resembled a giant bag, was sewn up, leaving the top still open, it was turned inside out and lathered with carbolic soap as a kind of waxing treatment; pillows and cushions made in the same fashion were treated likewise. This prevented the feathers from later breaking through the ticking. Then the tick was righted and filled with goose and duck down held over from the Christmas plucking. This was a sneeze-inducing, itchy business that involved carefully controlling your movements to avoid a feather snowstorm. A sudden breeze was highly undesirable and if anyone opened a door and created a draught they could be the victim of a disapproving tirade. When all the feathers were securely imprisoned within, the tick was firmly hand-stitched across the top with a good strong needle and heavy thread. It was then laid on top of the horsehair mattress on the spring base of the bed. Diving into bed on top of a newly filled feather tick was a child's delight – better than any bouncy castle.

The undertaking that caused the most excitement was the creation of an entire new christening outfit. This was a rare occurrence that only happened when a pregnant neighbour did not already have a family christening gown or when a discerning grandmother wanted to create a beautiful new family heirloom. Either way, Aunt Kate's visit afforded the opportunity to clothe the next generation with the skills of the past. On her arrival, she advised on the purchase of the required material and threads, and when they came there was much oohing and aahing amongst the women about the delicacy of the fabrics. Aunt Kate did the cutting out and under her guidance other women with the required skills did the needful. But Aunt Kate took charge of the finer details of embroidery and lace edging, and when the entire ensemble of gown, shawl, bonnet and bootees was complete it was a thing of beauty destined to become a family treasure for generations to come.

We loved it when Aunt Kate came to stay and by the time

she departed we were stitched up, darned in and togged out for the months ahead. Her trunk was returned to the attic in a much lighter condition. Her accomplishments enriched her life, our lives and those of our neighbours.

To this day at antique fairs I make a beeline for the linen table and cannot resist beautifully embroidered cloths of all shapes and sizes. She introduced one of my sisters to tapestry, which began a lifelong love affair. Our love of beautiful things all began with Aunt Kate when she turned our parlour into an Aladdin's cave and inspired her young charges and the neighbours to enjoy the art of creating beauty in everyday things.

Chapter 4

The Handy Woman

She had no qualifications other than her own experience, and her credentials would never be found in a modern CV. Her title could be hereditary, as she sometimes walked in the footprints of a wise mother who passed down her expertise from years of caring for the sick, delivering babies and laying out the dead. Because she delivered babies and laid out the dead, the Handy Woman was in touch with the two great realities of life, and over the years this had endowed her with a deep wisdom about the world and a great awareness of a world beyond. She lived in the midst of her community and was well versed in everybody's idiosyncrasies. But she was also involved in more everyday activities. At the time most women sewed and knitted for their own families, but if some found it beyond their capabilities the Handy Woman came to the rescue and added to her budget by doing the needful. She was not averse to going into a neighbouring house and taking on a tubful of washing to strengthen her family finances. When a pig was killed she helped with the filling of the puddings, at the threshing she was there to help feed the crowd at a *meitheal*, and she also helped to prepare for the Stations when major cleaning and cooking were done. Money did not always change hands, but fresh pork-steak, bacon, puddings, potatoes, milk and cabbage moved between houses.

Our local Handy Woman lived just beside us and she was present at all our family occasions. Her opinion carried great weight in any decision-making. Because she was involved in all our births, she had a big say in the choosing of names and if she considered a family name to be fading into oblivion she often rescued a forgotten ancestor from falling off the family tree. She would never have understood the practice of choosing celebrity names or 'unusual' names for children. As far as she was concerned a child was part of a family and should be christened accordingly. In one sentence she changed my name from my father's choice of Susan to Alice with the proclamation: 'Alice is an old Taylor name and if you don't call her that it will die out of the family.' And I became Alice because our Handy Woman so decided! The previous Alice was a great-aunt of my father's and so the Handy Woman reached well back into our ancestry to rescue that long-forgotten lady from the family archives. Years later when I decided to try to trace the family tree, I discovered the wisdom of the Handy Woman – when you are wading through reams of old records family names are like identifying stepping stones that guide you back through the generations. Now whole TV programmes are based on tracing who you think you are; in her time our Handy Woman laid down the guiding markers for identifying family lineage through successive generations.

She had an acre attached to her cottage and every inch of that acre was used to help feed her family. It had the grazing of two cows and when the grass supply dwindled, the cows were turned out to graze the sides of the ditches along the road. This was commonly called the 'long acre'. Her two pigs lived in an old wreck of a Baby Ford car minus the seats. How she acquired one of these when cars were as scarce as hen's teeth beggars belief. But the two pigs roamed the yard behind the cottage and at night squatted down comfortably in the Baby Ford. In the morning when hunger pangs surfaced they stuck their heads out the window and squealed for attention. Beside the pigs' car was a small house full of hens and ducks, and adjoining it a stone stable for the pony. The pony was tackled up to a tub-trap to take her and the family to Mass every Sunday; or to a cart to take milk to the creamery; or sometimes the cart was converted into a crib by adding slatted sides, making it safe to transport *bonhams* to the fair, or bring turf from the bog, where she went every year to cut her own.

She grew all her own potatoes and vegetables and if she ran out of ground she moved into one of our adjoining fields and made good this arrangement by helping us with cutting the corn and saving the hay. It wasn't that she had no husband – she did – she was simply an independent-minded woman too vigorous to follow anybody. She led, always. The husband worked on the roads with the County Council, but it was she, with all her industry, who truly kept the home fires burning. With no social welfare to back her up, this resourcefulness meant a well-clothed and well-fed family. She had never heard of women's liberation, but she was a liberated woman in her own way, believing that women were far more resourceful than men.

She reared strong independent daughters and when one of them came for a short time to help my mother she taught my father a sharp lesson. He had five daughters who were there to look after him and save him any domestic chores, he believed – and that included bringing the teapot from the open fire to the table when he needed a cup of tea! Shortly after the arrival of the Handy Woman's daughter he asked her to bring over the teapot. She coolly eyeballed him and promptly told him to do it himself. We thought this was hilarious! Years afterwards when she came back to visit us, she and my father both laughed heartily at his abrupt introduction to the new world.

My father had huge respect for the Handy Woman and often regaled us with stories about her. Once she and her husband were out in our Brake Field where they were digging their own potatoes. Normally, in these circumstances, the man would do the digging with a spade and the woman would follow on with the bucket, picking up the potatoes. But with the Handy Woman the situation was reversed. She did the digging and he did the picking. It told a lot about their relationship. On this particular day she had gone far up the field ahead of him and when my father went to chat with her she looked back at her husband and with very little sympathy in her voice pronounced acidly, 'My little man is failing.' My father continued down the field to the husband who, with a knowing expression on his face, looked up the field at his wife and told my father, 'I let her forge ahead or otherwise she might think that she was failing.' They certainly had the measure of each other!

The Handy Woman did not trust modern medicine and believed firmly in her own home cures. She was into doing everything naturally, from childbirth to death. On top of all her home industry she was always on call for home births and for laying out the dead. Before the era of the District Nurse, she did the baby deliveries. When the District Nurse was appointed she continued to help, but there could be a bit of a power struggle between them. Sometimes if babies moved faster than expected and came before the arrival of the Nurse, the Handy Woman was delighted to be the one to have seen the new baby into the world, while also taking good care of the mother. A staunch believer in breast feeding, she advised all new mothers that apart from being good for the baby it was far handier, and she advised the new mother to have a soothing nightcap of a warm bottle of stout; this would guarantee both mother and baby a sound night's sleep.

She absolutely loved babies and thought that children could do no wrong, and if they were less than perfect she judged it to be the fault of the parents. Where the 'terrible twos' were concerned she dished out advice too, declaring that it was best not to 'cross them' but to let them work out their tantrums in their own time. She told worried mothers to relax and that the children would eventually figure it all out for themselves. If adult behaviour was less than honourable she would remark sagely, 'Some day their own will level them; it always takes your own to level you.'

As well as home births it was also the time of home deaths. Most people died in their own beds, and wakes were held in the family home. As soon as a death took place the Handy Woman was summoned and from years of experience she knew exactly what to do. Because she had known the deceased all their lives she undertook this act of preparation for their final journey as a great honour and performed it with loving kindness. Her aim was to make them look as well as possible, but this was the era before magic makeovers, and none of them looked as if they were about to go partying.

When an old neighbour Mike died, she was called by his two sisters to lay him out. She had known him all her life. All went according to plan until she looked for his hat. Mike had always worn his hat, even in bed. Few people had ever seen Mike without his hat on. So the Handy Woman felt that it was only right and proper that he should go to meet his maker wearing his hat. Mike, she decided, would feel bare without it. But the hat had disappeared. In preparation for the wake his two house-proud sisters had done a big tidying-up job and Mike's hat had got whipped out of sight and was nowhere to be seen. But our Handy Woman was resourceful in all situations so she searched the wardrobe of the wake room and found a classy black hat belonging to one of the sisters – and she did a quick Philip Treacy job on it. Because she was an able seamstress she quickly turned the sister's fashionable hat into a replica of Mike's own hat. She popped it on his head and nobody knew the difference. But when the funeral was leaving the house his sister went in search of her hat that was nowhere to be found …

Wakes could go on for a few days and without the aid of modern body preservatives she kept a watchful eye over her charge until they made it safely out of the bed into the coffin and were on the final journey.

Our Handy Woman and her little cottage are long gone, but hopefully when she arrived wherever it is we are all going she was welcomed home by the many neighbours that she had fitted out for their journey.

Chapter 5

The District Nurse

Known simply as 'The Nurse', her name was breathed with the same air of respect as if she were the Queen of England or the President of Ireland. This respect was due to the significance of her role in the community. She was appointed to the district to replace the 'Handy Woman', who up to then had overseen the home births. She was the first female qualified medical practitioner to find her way into the homes of rural Ireland. Other nurses earned their wages in hospitals caring for strangers, but the Nurse earned the respect of the whole parish by bringing most of them into the world and then keeping a motherly eye on them. She exuded capability and tranquility. Her very presence calmed frayed nerves. If you were deemed to be running out of steam, the Nurse and doctor came to your aid, but whereas the doctor diagnosed and departed, the Nurse continued to call until you were back on your feet. She had years of experience under her belt, and with so much knowledge of her community she was often more astute than any doctor in analysing a complaint. She usually initiated new young GPs, who were then always men, into the intricacies of rural medical care. She knew the seed and breed of the whole parish and was familiar with the health weaknesses of different families. She had a basic knowledge of the frailties of the various branches in everyone's family tree. She knew, for example, from years of recurring kidney complaints, that the Browns had bad plumbing but that their leaky water system was nothing to get alarmed about as most of them drained away into their late nineties. She also knew that the O'Learys had the constitution of horses and if one of them went down it was serious business requiring drastic action.

Often her ears had access to secrets usually heard only in the confessional, and in rows between neighbours she often built bridges with the bones of hidden skeletons in the cupboard, known only to her. Sometimes, driven to desperation, she quietly told troublesome husbands that she had brought them into the world and that if she had been blessed with foresight she might well have deemed that a drowning in their bath water would have made the world a better place! Strong-willed men nodded respectfully when she begged to differ with their rigidly held opinions.

The Nurse was on duty day and night, and while she was available to cure complaints of all kinds her top priority was in the baby production line. She loved her mothers and babies. They were her pride and joy. Before babies were heralded into the world by gynaecologists in the antiseptic realms of hospitals, the Nurse travelled around the parish where home births were still part of the way of life. Her means of transport was her bike on which she carried her 'bag of tricks', as some disrespectful new fathers termed her bag of medical instruments.

Often she was collected late at night by a stressed expectant father. The mode of transport then could be a posh pony and trap borne along by a well-trained pony in top-class brass and leather tackling, but it could also be a kicking horse hastily tackled to a cart, or indeed a battered butt. As well as the hazards of the protesting horse, the butt might not be too clean, but it was all that was available on the night. Sometimes the butt that came to collect her had some of the base boards missing so the Nurse had to be careful lest she fell down through the gaps. On rare occasions she had to get up onto the back of a startled horse behind an anxious farmer and cling on for dear life as they made their way to the waiting mother. But she took all this in her stride. She understood her people and knew that times were hard. If a particular call was to a family in dire straits she came with her own towels and extra bedlinen. She was ready for any emergency. In her world the care of mother and baby were the top priority. Because money was scarce she was not always paid in cash, but bags of turf, potatoes and vegetables or plucked chickens frequently found their way to her door.

On her arrival she went immediately to the birthing room. This could be the parlour, which was temporarily turned into a labour ward because it was the largest room in the house, or it could be the main bedroom. Here the maternal grandmother was usually in residence. The birthing room was strictly a female domain and all males were evicted, including the expectant father, who the Nurse felt had already made his contribution – and sometimes a little more often than was necessary! The Nurse might talk to him about that later as natural family planning was not outside her brief – but that was for another day. Now the father's function was to keep his mouth shut, boil water and provide it on demand.

The comfort and support of the mother in labour was the Nurse's all-prevailing concern. She talked and soothed and if it was a first-time mother she advised on positioning, coping with pain and pushing. If it was a long labour, tea was brought to the room by the grandmother, who also brought in the hot water. As the labour became more intense, the Nurse supported the mother at one side of the bed and the grandmother did the same at the other side. During these hours of sometimes excruciating pressure the women worked in harmony to ride the waves of contractions as they came and went. Screams of pain and prayers blended with the sprinkling of holy water as the women bonded to bring new life into the world. Finally, in a crescendo of agony and ecstasy, a baby slid into life. If the delivery did not go according to plan the doctor was summoned, and gas and air came into action to ease the situation. But generally the women saw the whole delivery through to the end. The knowledgeable Nurse checked that all was well with the new baby and after other practicalities were seen to and the mother made comfortable, the father was invited in to see the new arrival.

Also waiting in the kitchen could be the paternal grandmother and aunts, uncles and close neighbours. Sometimes while the labour went on, the rosary was recited for a safe delivery. Birthing was a family affair.

After the safe arrival, a discussion might take place as to the naming of the new baby. If it was a first baby the name of the paternal grandparent was always on the agenda and for a second baby the other side of the house could be invoked. After that, various options came up for debate and the family tree was sourced for any overlooked ancestors whose name needed to be renewed. At the time it was considered very important to know who it was you were 'called after'. In some way you felt connected to them, and it was also thought that this strengthened the branches of the family tree and tied the family more closely together. The Nurse sat through many of these discussions, but, unlike her predecessor the Handy Woman, she seldom voiced her opinion, though if she did, she was always listened to carefully.

The christening took place within days and the new mother did not attend because she was still house-bound. She was confined to bed for ten days to two weeks and during that time the Nurse came daily to check that all was well with her and her baby. The Nurse also cast a caring eye over the other children in the house. When my baby brother was born I was suffering from an ear infection and every morning my ear was moist with discharge. The Nurse tackled my complaint with ear drops which she inserted on her daily visits. After a few mornings my ear was dry and I was very excited to report success. I was only two then, so the image of the Nurse must be one of my earliest memories. That memory is vague and misty, but I recall being curled up in the well of the window watching her talking to my mother and examining the new baby, and it was morning because the cows were out in the field below the house. Childhood has a long memory.

Years later when I came into my own baby-production phase the District Nurse in our village had retired and babies were making their debut in the antiseptic hallowed halls of the Bon Secours Maternity Hospital in Cork, where I was installed for a week. But when I brought my first-born home I too benefited from the Nurse's experience and love of babies. Every morning on her way home from Mass she called in and bathed my baby. I was immensely grateful because as a new, inexperienced mother I was afraid I might inadvertently drown, choke or smother this new miracle in our midst. The Nurse sailed in the door exuding confidence and tranquility and effortlessly executed what I considered a gigantic and terrifying undertaking. As soon as she arrived I felt better and I could well understand how in bygone days her arrival at the home of a mother in labour calmed frayed nerves. For me her presence was like an Indian head massage, one of my favourite forms of relaxation!

One morning, having bathed and bedded the new arrival, she and I sat having tea and chatting about her life as the Nurse. She told me that as soon as a woman became pregnant she called to the Nurse to discuss her situation, and throughout her pregnancy the Nurse came regularly to check on her progress. When I asked what home births were like she smiled in warm remembrance and told me simply, 'They were great women', and she repeated this constantly during our conversation. It was obvious that she had immense respect for 'my mothers', as she referred to them. 'Had you any painkillers?' I enquired. 'Ah no,' she said

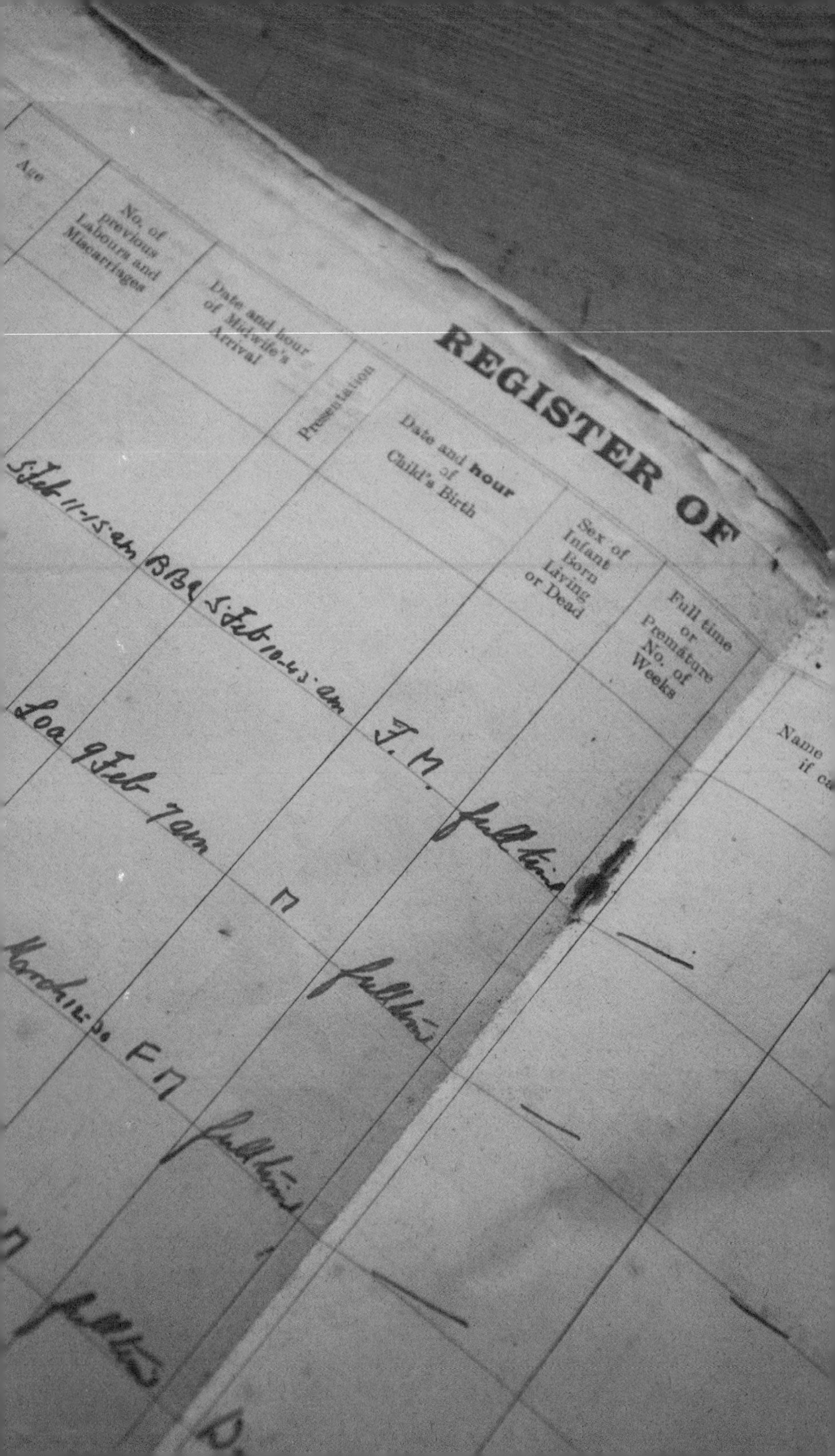

REGISTER OF
Age
No. of previous Labours and Miscarriages
Date and hour of Midwife's Arrival
Presentation
Date and hour of Child's Birth
Sex of Infant Born Living or Dead
Full time or Premature No. of Weeks

quietly, 'sure, we didn't need them. We prayed.' With the excruciating pains of first childbirth still fresh in my mind, I was not at all sure that the power of prayer would have got me through my ordeal. I fully agreed with her pronouncement that they were great women.

But although she did not dispense any painkillers she alleviated pain in her own way and brought great comfort and security to her mothers because she soothed, instructed, encouraged and always prayed. 'The mothers prayed too,' she said, 'and sometimes we prayed together and it all helped, but for everything I trusted in God. I always felt close to God in my work and over the years He always helped me to get to my mothers when they needed me.'

She told me that in 1930 she had trained as a midwife in the Coombe Hospital in Dublin and her first appointment was to a maternity hospital in Lower Leeson Street where she got valuable experience which she put into practice when she moved to Cork, where she joined the staff of St Kevin's Nursing Home in South Terrace. Later she returned to her native Bandon, where she worked in what was called the 'Miss Beamish Home', after its matron. In 1943 a vacancy arose for a District Nurse in our village of Innishannon and she was appointed.

It was plain to see that the Nurse had loved her job and that for her the special joy of welcoming a new baby had never faded throughout the years. When I asked about the modern perception of the dangers of home births she smiled softly and said, 'I brought seven hundred babies into the world and never lost a baby or a mother.' What a wonderful achievement, and it was no wonder that at the end of her days the Nurse could look back with satisfaction on a job well done. During our conversation she had constantly proclaimed that her mothers were great women. But I knew that I was talking to a great woman!

Chapter 6

The Road from Puck

Whenever they were camped down by the bridge, Maggie May called to our house to collect food and clothes for her children. There was often a baby sheltering beneath her shawl. She lived on the side of the road in a horse-drawn caravan with her husband and six children. They had no regular income and no social welfare, of course. Her husband Jimmy dealt in horses but often drank the money and she struggled to feed her family with door-to-door begging and selling religious trinkets, mothballs, paper flowers and clothes pegs from a basket. At different fairs around the country she told fortunes. Her mother had taught her how to read palms and sometimes she surprised people by what she was able to reveal.

Her husband's father travelled with them in a cart drawn by a piebald pony and at night he pitched his canvas tent on the ground between the shafts of the cart. It was a cold, hard bed but he never complained. He was a chimney sweep and he also still practised the old tinsmith's skills that had earned their people the name 'Tinkers'.

It was a hard life and Maggie May wanted better for her children. Usually she called to our house after the dinner when the men had gone back out to the fields, and my mother gave her her dinner. One day as they sat talking, she told my mother about her struggle for survival, a struggle shared by many women living in difficult circumstances. She also spoke of her hopes for the future. I was listening and never forgot. This is Maggie May's story.

* * *

'Man mind thyself and woman mind the children.' Maggie May mumbled her mother's oft-quoted philosophy as she clustered her children behind her into the safety of the pub doorway. This horse-fair day invariably ended in a drunken brawl. Some bare-chested traveller men and a few diehard locals belted each other around the centre of the town. Their quick-thinking wives took advantage of the situation to help themselves to the forgotten money in their menfolk's abandoned jackets – money that earlier in the day had been extracted from tight-fisted farmers after hours of arguing, horse tangling, back slapping, palm spitting and much walking to and fro until an agreement was hammered out.

She had watched as Jimmy had argued and tangled all morning with a miserable old bachelor farmer from up the hill behind the sheltered corner where they were now camped. She knew that if old Paddy was too tight-fisted with Jimmy, tomorrow night Jimmy would even the score by opening a gate at night and letting their pony graze in Paddy's best field. Paddy knew this as well and the unspoken agenda brokered a fair deal. She smiled in satisfaction when their cob mare fetched a good price. It would keep hunger at bay for the coming winter – that was if Jimmy did not flitter it away in Kitty Mac's pub that evening. That was always the problem with Jimmy, once he got into a pub he lost the head and their money disappeared in over the pub counter faster than water down a hill. And it wasn't always spent on himself but often on hangers-on who knew that once he was tanked up Jimmy acted as if he had money to burn.

Then a chance to prevent this calamity presented itself when an old sparring partner landed a right upper cut on Jimmy's jaw and sent him sprawling. Recalling her mother's attitude, she put the eldest, Kate, in charge of the other children, then slipped down the street to Jimmy's abandoned jacket and helped herself to most of the roll of money bulging from the inside pocket. She quickly pushed the wad of notes up the leg of her knickers and beckoning the children to follow she headed out of town. As they scrambled to catch up with her, Kate asked, 'Where you going to hide it, Ma?' 'None of your business, child, better not to know.' 'Will you get away with it?' Packie asked. 'I'll handle that,' she said in a voice that threatened no squealing on her.

Later, when the children were bedded down for the night, she slipped down the steps of the caravan and walked along by the ditch to where the old man had his makeshift camp between the shafts of his cart. 'Will you mind it?' she asked. 'Of course,' and the brown gnarled hand reached out through a flap in the canvas tent. She handed him the roll of notes. He was Jimmy's father, but there was bad blood between them. Her mother had warned her to be careful: 'Bad blood between father and son is never good.' She had never been told the full story of the old man but she knew that there was something about a knife fight in a pub in London and that he had served time. It had turned him into a loner and people were afraid to cross swords with him.

But she found that the bad blood between father and son worked to her advantage and early in her marriage she became aware that the old man was on her side. Jimmy was afraid of his father and it was good that he was afraid of someone because when he got in a rage he could wreck the caravan and beat them all. But the old man would have none of it. Nothing was ever said, but the old man would sense when a storm was brewing and quell it before it gained full force. This understanding worked to both the old man's advantage and Maggie May's. She fed him and he minded the money and Jimmy never knew a thing about it.

The old man was a chimney sweep and every year, once Puck was over, they all moved from valley to valley where people waited for him to clean their chimneys. He spoke very little, but for some reason that she could never quite fathom, the settled people treated him with far more respect than they did Jimmy. He carried his chimney sticks around in his cart and as she approached the cart now she could see them tied up firmly in black bundles at the bottom of the shallow cart.

With the money safe, she continued walking until she reached a rusty gate. She climbed over it, tossed off her boots and headed down towards the river. It was great to feel the soft, moist, dewy grass under her feet. The freedom of bare feet after the constraining feel of battered old boots was wonderful. She seldom had comfortable shoes or boots to wear – only the leftovers that others had already moulded into the shape of their feet. She gathered them on the door-to-door begging and when people gave them away they were always well worn. The only time they got good footwear was when someone died; Jimmy called it 'wearing dead man's boots'. But she didn't care once they provided a bit of comfort.

As she walked along she sniffed the lovely smell of the

night. The cows lying contentedly chewing the cud around the field looked at her calmly as if she was one of them. Pity, she thought, that some farmers were not more like their cows. It was a warm night and a long sunny summer had lulled her into thinking that she loved this way of life. And in many ways she did, but the winters were rough and it was hard on the children, though looking back to when she was a child she had never thought of it as hard. She had accepted that this was her life and she loved the freedom. It was only as she grew older and less able to cope with the hardships that she wanted things to change. But as a child she had enjoyed it and when she went begging with her mother up to some of the little houses in the mountains she could see that some people there were no better off than they were. But though these people were poor they were still tempted by the colourful contents of her mother's basket. They bought the little holy pictures, mothballs and paper flowers and her mother always came home in the evening with money at the bottom of her basket.

Down in the valleys where the land was good the people were different. Some of the farmers' wives were generous and gave them leftover dinners, but some banged the door in their faces and threatened them with their dogs. But over the years she saw that her mother had grown to know the valley people and she treated with respect the people who treated them well. But she was mean to the people who were mean

to them. Often on the way out of a farmyard where they had been badly treated her mother would call to the henhouses and would help herself to eggs from the nests, or, indeed, sometimes put a fine fat young hen under her shawl. That night they would have roast chicken for dinner.

But what she envied the settled people most was the roof over their heads in winter. On freezing cold winter nights when her teeth chattered under bare blankets, she envied them their warm beds. But on warm balmy summer days as she travelled from place to place, she was glad to be out on the road and free. Yet this meant that she had never learned to read and write and now in middle age she realised that this was a big disadvantage. She had never been in any place long enough to go to school. When she protested to Jimmy about their children not going to school he turned a deaf ear. And, of course, they agreed with him as they had no desire to be locked up all day. So the odds were stacked against her. But she was determined that in some way or other she would get them some schooling and she knew that the old man agreed with her in this.

When she got back to the caravan Jimmy was asleep at the bottom of the steps. He had obviously tried to climb up but was too drunk to make it and was now face downwards on the ground. She stepped over him and went up the ladder and shut the door firmly behind her. A night out in the open air would do him no harm, she decided.

The following morning when he was still there she shook him awake and catching him by the collar of his shirt demanded, 'Where is the money?' 'What money are you talking about, woman?' he spluttered, trying to gather his clouded wits about him. 'The money for the cob,' she shouted, backing him up against the side of the caravan. A foggy remembrance ebbed into his eyes but she could see that the previous night was lost in a haze. Still, she was determined to hammer home her advantage just in case he would wonder why she was not raging mad over the loss of the money.'Where is it?' she blazed, slapping him hard across the face. This was a step too far and Jimmy lunged at her, but she was too adroit for him and he fell over the steps and lay cursing on the ground.

Kate was in the caravan taking it all in and Maggie May knew that the young girl was learning the rules of survival for the road, as she had learned from her own mother. But she was hoping that Kate was also learning that there could be a better way. Some day, by hook or by crook, she was going to get Kate to school. That would open the door for the others.

Chapter 7

The Chapel Woman

Ellie inherited the job from her sister Nonie, who had inherited it from their mother. How their mother became the Chapel Woman in the first place could have had something to do with the fact that they lived on Chapel Hill in the house nearest to the church. Nonie regarded it as an honour as much as a job. As well as cleaning the church and sacristy, she looked after the altar linen and brasses, which was no small job with so many ceremonies held in those days. She resisted strongly when a modern-thinking priest tried to put the whole arrangement on a more business-like basis and give her a proper wage and pay insurance for her and stamp her card. To Nonie this was lowering her vocation to a mere job. She was a fine-boned stooped little

lady who carried in her head the site map of the graveyard surrounding the church. Priests came and went, but the Chapel Woman went on for ever. She knew where we were all buried and directed grave diggers to the right spot. Once, due to misunderstood instructions, a coffin went into the wrong grave and the following day she had it dug up quietly and put in the correct location. She was respectful and deferential to the priest and almost genuflected to the bishop.

But her sister, Ellie, was a different cup of tea altogether! When Nonie became crippled with arthritis Ellie moved in and took over. They were two very different women, both mentally and physically. Whereas Nonie was small, frail and self-effacing, Ellie was a tall, strong, forthright woman with a fine head of chestnut brown hair flecked with grey. Her husband had died and she had no children, so she felt free to come back to help Nonie for a while. It was always supposed to be a temporary arrangement but over the years it evolved into a permanent one. To Ellie, the church had to be taken care of to the best of her ability, but she took no nonsense from anyone, including the priests. Yet beneath her gruff exterior and forthright manner she was quick-witted, droll and funny. She was very deaf, but you could carry on a long conversation with her without becoming aware of the fact. Whether she lip-read or simply guessed what it was you were saying you were never quite sure.

Part of the front room of their little house had been turned into a sweet shop and as the school was farther up the hill beyond the church there was a constant flow of children straining up to the high counter to reach across with big brown pennies in pursuit of toffee bars, Black Jacks, Love Hearts and Peggy's Legs. Ellie took over that job from Nonie too and enjoyed chatting with the children. Another job she inherited was the daily opening and maintenance of the dispensary, where the doctor saw his patients. Slowly over the years, Nonie's arthritis worsened and she was confined to a wheelchair, so Ellie's workload increased. By then Ellie was into her eighties but she still continued doggedly with the same routine.

She opened the church before half-past-eight Mass every morning and had all in readiness when the priest arrived. If he happened to run late she made him aware that it was hardly good enough! The altar boys were trained by her and she lined them up like small soldiers and put manners on any little guy who thought that he had the right to do it his way. She made sure that their altar clothes were kept in good order and insisted that they wear special canvas sandals while serving Mass. The First Communion children were lined up to her satisfaction on their big day and any unseemly behaviour by an overenthusiastic camera-happy parent was frowned on. When the bishop came for Confirmation, she felt that it was up to him to accommodate her rather than expecting her to rush around trying to have things organised to his satisfaction. She took all the fuss accompanying weddings in her stride but took a very dim view of the bride who removed all the flowers when the ceremony was over. The graveyard also came under her jurisdiction and she loved it when people took good care of their grave. Like Nonie, she too had a map of the graveyard in her head. If a family failed to maintain the family grave she would shake her head in disgust saying, 'That woman thought she reared them well and now there she is, after all she did for them, and she's buried in weeds.'

She looked after Nonie with firm kindness. Sometimes Nonie would forget that their younger brother was dead and would lay the table for three. When Ellie arrived back from locking up the church this would annoy her intensely and she would demand, 'Who is that third setting for?' 'Jimmy,' Nonie would tell her vaguely. 'For God's sake, woman, that man is dead with ten years. Do you think he's going to rise up and come down from the graveyard to have tea with us?' In this way she brought Nonie back to reality and for years kept her anchored in the real world. She would not allow Nonie to get lost in a world of confusion and would sit down and talk her back into their world.

As long as I knew her, Ellie wore the same long fawn gabardine coat and a strong pair of brown leather laced-up shoes. For Mass, this was topped with a round brown hat with a dull velvet ribbon that was more sensible than stylish. Everything about Ellie was solid and practical, with no pretensions. One day while walking up the hill with her I remarked, 'Ellie, you carry an amazing workload.' 'One day,' she told me, 'I will drop down stone cold dead and that will be that.' And that was exactly what happened. One morning we arrived to find the church still locked and it set alarm bells ringing: there could only be one reason – Ellie had to be out of action. Indeed, she had got a heart attack and was rushed to hospital where she died that evening.

Her death triggered off a whole chain reaction of events. There was no one to look after Nonie, who went into a nursing home, where, without Ellie to keep her connected, she quickly lost touch with reality. The little sweet shop closed and there was no one to look after the dispensary. And for the church it was the end of an era. Ellie was the last Chapel Woman.

Fr Seamus, who was then curate and who was extremely fond of her despite all her idiosyncrasies, said her funeral Mass. For many of us present it was difficult to imagine that her solid brown figure would never again plod down the altar steps and plonk herself into the front seat where she had kept an alert eye on her altar boys, and indeed on Fr Seamus as well. On her coffin was a wreath given by a Church of Ireland neighbour with the inscription: 'Well done, thou good and faithful servant.' It was a fitting tribute.

After the funeral an old friend of Ellie's asked me to tidy out their house with her. We arrived with buckets and brushes expecting a straightforward sorting and cleaning job. But a surprise awaited us. In drawers and under mattresses all around the house were rolls and rolls of bank notes. We were flabbergasted. Where had all the money come from? But then we sat down and reasoned it out. Ellie and Nonie had lived thriftily all their lives. They knew no other way and even when their incomes increased with their old age pensions, it made no difference to their spending. So they simply rolled up the money and put it by and over the years they simply forgot all about it. They were not mean but just had never mastered the art of spending.

Over the years they had had many visitors with whom they walked the graveyard to locate ancestors. But one visitor who came had no blood connection whatsoever with them or our village. Nonie and Ellie had an older brother who had emigrated to America, and one day in the early seventies a young student who lived next door to him and his wife came to visit the sisters. She was a beautiful young girl and because Nonie and Ellie had limited accommodation she stayed with me. She became good friends with Fr Seamus and his young housekeeper Joan, who was about her own age. Until the sisters died, this young girl returned many times to visit them and even when they were gone she continued to return to visit their grave behind the

Chapter 8

To the Manor Born

We Irish are not part of the stiff-upper-lip brigade, as our Celtic bloodline renders us prone to ride high and low waves of emotional roller-coasters. Our British next-door neighbours, with their Saxon origins, maintain a far more controlled voyage as they journey through life. Maybe it explains the clash of personality between our two nations and the reason why the English have always found it so difficult to understand the 'Irish problem', as they termed it. When the two nations blended, the result was the Anglo-Irish, whom the English considered Irish and the Irish considered English. But the mixture resulted in an interesting blend of two cultures.

My closest experience of the Anglo-Irish culture was

when 'Mrs C' (Mrs Cummings) came to live under our roof – I can't remember why we shortened her name but we always called her Mrs C. Her father had represented the West of Ireland at Westminster and she had been reared in one of the great houses in the west. But years before our paths crossed I got to know a previous husband of hers when he purchased a house down the river from our village. He was a large, dashing, handsome, bearded man, who lived a flamboyant lifestyle and bore a strong resemblance to Clark Gable. A whiff of romantic danger accompanied him when he whizzed down the steep incline in his low-slung open-roofed car from his riverside pad into the village. In keeping with his bohemian lifestyle, a beautiful blonde was a regular visitor, but a few years after his sudden demise two different families emerged from his colourful past.

The son of his first wife took care of all the funeral arrangements and in the process we got to know a quiet-spoken gentle young man who, apart from a slight physical resemblance, could have come from a different planet to his father. I decided there and then that he must be like his mother, whom I had never met – not yet. This young man inherited his father's beautiful riverside home and I discovered that his father had been the second husband of his mother. One sensed the parting was not very amicable. This wonderful young man must have inherited the best qualities of both parents because when he stayed in our guest house over the period of the funeral he poured tranquility on troubled family waters and built sensitive bridges between all the assembled, somewhat confusing, branches. Funeral over, he returned to London and rented out his house down the river.

A few years later I received a letter from a woman in Switzerland booking a room in our guest house and it mentioned that she was the mother of this gentle young man. Finally, I thought, I am to meet the woman who was married to our dashing Clark Gable. At our first meeting the image of Wallis Simpson immediately came to mind – a pencil-slim immaculately dressed lady of Parisian elegance. She was accompanied by a pleasant, amiable husband; one would imagine life might be a lot less stressful with him than with the late Clark Gable. They were a charming couple and as this husband worked for the UN they had lived in many countries. Now he was about to retire and they planned to move into her son's house down the river.

So they came to Innishannon and lived for a number of years in their lovely home where they entertained and gardened in blissful harmony until one sunny morning he got a heart attack and died suddenly, leaving Mrs C alone in her beautiful but isolated home. We assumed that she would return to her family in London. Her much-loved son, who had a wonderful wife with whom she got on well, lived there and there was also an adult daughter of her recently deceased husband with whom she had a very amicable relationship. But as I was to learn in later years, with Mrs C you always had to expect the unexpected.

A few weeks after the funeral, when the extended family had returned to their various locations, she called to see me to inquire if it would be possible for her to move into our 'west wing'. Due to family commitments we no longer ran a guest house, but at the end of one upstairs corridor we had converted three small rooms into a little self-contained apartment. It consisted of a tiny sitting room, kitchen and bedroom – and one satirical son had christened it the 'west wing'.

The idea that Mrs C would move in here, even temporarily, after the living accommodation to which she was accustomed came as a bit of a surprise. This, I decided, would be a short-term arrangement until she got her affairs in order and moved back to England. But she stoically downsized, selling off her lovely furniture, and moved into the little apartment upstairs. She decorated it to her own taste and brought with her some of her most treasured pieces. What she found most difficult to leave behind were her beloved books, of which she could only bring a limited number. But she came to grips with her new situation with admirable determination – and stiff upper lip – and was soon ensconced in her new corner. After a few weeks she inquired about installing a telephone, and I realised that Mrs C was here to stay.

I wondered, was this really going to work out? Would she be able to cope with living long-term in such confined quarters? What I had not realised was that Mrs C was moulded from stern stuff! During the following fourteen years that she lived in the midst of our often chaotic household, my admiration for her grew as I watched her resilience and coping skills unfold. She kept in touch with all her old friends, whom she entertained in her small kitchen-cum-dining room as if it were the Ritz. Some of these friends were titled faded aristocracy and none was in the first flush of youth. After dinner in her little corner, the aroma of brandy and cigars often wafted along the corridor and I would smile, thinking that this was a real 'Upstairs Downstairs' scenario.

She was wonderful company and had a wicked sense of humour. Once when I remarked about all the effort she put into entertaining her friends she told me, 'I don't always enjoy it, you know my dear, but one has to bring one's penny to the pool and keep one's brain alive.' Keeping her brain alive was high on her list of priorities and every day she got her special newspaper that had a seriously challenging crossword, and she grappled with it throughout the day, poring over her dense dictionary until she had finally cracked it. If you called in to see her, she tested your crossword expertise. She watched every sport on TV and kept a close eye on local and world politics. She told me that she abhorred the burning of the great houses, including her own, during what were with scant regard for the correct time, but they were swiftly dismissed, dispatched downstairs and told to come up at the agreed time. She abhorred the Irish lack of correct time-keeping. Her bedtime and rising time were like clockwork, and, as we downstairs were a late-to-bed brigade, she regularly informed me that 'The Irish are too lazy to go to bed', a pronouncement that I now often call to mind when I am reluctant to rise from the couch late at night and get myself upstairs. A morning lie-in was not on her agenda either as I discovered one cold January morning, with snow on the ground, when I went upstairs with her daily papers. 'You should stay in bed for a while,' I advised her. 'It's a bitter morning.' 'My dear,' she told me firmly, 'that is the last thing that I propose to do. With your lifestyle you cannot have a lie-in and when you do it's a luxury. You have to get up the following morning. But I do not have to get up any morning, so I must! Staying in bed is the thin edge of the wedge and then it's down a slippery slope.'

Often at night I called up to her and she was full of interest in what was going on downstairs and indeed in all the village activities. One night she looked out her sitting-room window onto the village street where she observed an elderly man and woman go into the pub across the road. A few years previously they had moved in together, which had surprised many as he was a slightly doddering old bachelor and she too was well past the first flush of youth. 'Isn't that an interesting development, now,' she mused, 'but I doubt that she has him for his sexual prowess.' And I doubted that anyone else in the village had been bold enough to voice the complexities of the liaison from that angle.

As the frailties of old age took hold, she never indulged, as so many do, in the exercise of airing her medical complaints. One day when I remarked on that, she told me with conviction, 'My mother taught me that. She told me never to indulge in self-pity. It destroys yourself and annihilates people.' I had first-hand experience of the wisdom of that observation because staying with us at the time was a relative who was the same vintage as Mrs C but whose main interest in life was her pains and aches: the first thing on her agenda for every visitor was her medical report! The result was that visitors were scarce and our children, who were teenagers at the time, had to be corralled into visiting her downstairs bedroom, whereas Mrs C, who challenged and argued with them, was a constant source of interest. Like Oscar Wilde, Mrs C considered that the only unforgivable offence in life was to be boring, so she struggled gallantly against the frailties of old age and kept all flags flying.

She had a deep interest in art, and her final long-distance journey was a trip to Moscow to view Russian art. Hanging on the wall of her little sitting room was an original Jack Yeats painting; there was a family connection as her brother had been in school with the artist. While it hung there I savoured the experience of viewing it, knowing that I would never be the owner of such a significant original work.

Once when she had to go to hospital she decided on the Bon Secours, which she declared to be the only 'civilised' hospital in Cork. She instructed me to go out before the visit and purchase a pure silk nightdress. On her arrival home just before Christmas I assumed that she would lie low for a while to recover and was surprised one morning to meet her coming down the stairs very smartly dressed. 'Are you off to Cork shopping?' I enquired. 'Not at all,' she announced. 'I am going to Harrods to do my Christmas shopping.' From Innishannon!

A few years later, due to an unexpected illness, she had to go into a large city hospital. The consultant decided that the complaint was serious enough to warrant an overnight stay, but she was having none of it. 'Absolutely not,' she told him. 'This place is like the London Underground,' and promptly discharged herself, hiring a private ambulance to bring her back to Innishannon. I was summoned upstairs and asked to source a local nurse who would do the needful and also somebody to look after her little apartment. One of the pluses of village living is that you have knowledge and access to all sources of help within the community, and so Kitty and Phil came on board. Kitty looked after the apartment and Phil looked after Mrs C. We were blessed with both choices. Looking after the apartment was easy enough, but caring for Mrs C was a whole different ball game. But Phil was a born nurse and she and Mrs C got on extremely well, behaving like a mother and the daughter that Mrs C never had. Phil had the medical, spiritual and caring nature required in the circumstances and Mrs C was very appreciative of quality and knew that she was in the hands of a jewel.

When she died quietly we all missed her dreadfully. Because she was 'to the manor born' she had brought to the 'west wing' a sense of gracious living and good behaviour. And because she was so determined to keep her brain alive and 'bring her penny to the pool', it was always a place of good company. She left me with a sense of admiration for her indomitable spirit and a deep appreciation for her type of woman.

YARDLEY
Old English Lavender
TALC POWDER

Chapter 9

Faraway Places

On Sunday mornings they walked with orderly precision down the long winding avenue from the local convent, turned left up the steep incline of Main Street and into our parish church. Just before Mass they filed in military formation up the main aisle and edged demurely into the front rows of seats. Dozens of young fresh-faced girls wearing long-sleeved black dresses, well down below their knees, over black stockings and well-polished black shoes. The dresses were edged with white collars and cuffs. Well-trimmed hair was firmly held in place by hidden hair clips. They were the picture of dignity and decorum. Two brown-garbed nuns, with crackling white front pieces and white-edged brown capes above long rustling skirts and clinking rosary beads, brought up the rear and slipped into the seats behind them from where they could keep a supervisory eye on their charges. To me they were as intriguing as super beings from another planet. I loved to watch them arrive and never took my eyes off them for the entire Mass.

Their convent was an impressive lordly grey limestone mansion at the end of a long winding avenue surrounded by rolling fields and magnificent trees at the edge of our town. Since 1620 this impressive building had been the home of the Aldworth family. An interesting story from the house involves Lady Elizabeth St Leger of nearby Doneraile Court, who later became the wife of Sir Richard Aldworth. She was the only woman Freemason in the world. The Masons, a male-only secret society, were holding one of their meetings in a room in Doneraile Court, when Lady Mary, who was reading a book in an adjacent room with a connecting door, fell asleep. When she woke up she listened in on their meeting and then, realising the gravity of her situation, she tried to make a quiet exit, but they were alerted to her presence. The Masons had two choices: execute her or accept her into the Freemasons – and luckily for her they chose the latter.

The Aldworths were one of the many Anglo-Irish families who had graced and grazed the lands of Ireland until their situation became untenable when we decided that this land was our land. After the departure of the Aldworths, the Sisters of St Joseph took up residence in 1927. They were an

Australian order founded in 1866 by Mary Helen MacKillop, who became Sr Mary of the Cross and met much opposition from a male-dominated Church to her visionary venture of setting up an order of nuns to educate and care for poor children. But she persisted, and when she died in 1909 her order was well established throughout Australia. Her burning creed in life was: 'Never see a need without doing something about it.' The convent in Newmarket was a recruiting ground for Irish postulants for the houses in Australia and New Zealand, and the nuns there also taught music and ran a commercial school.

I never forgot those postulants, some of whom were not much older than I was, and I wondered how they had fared. Then in recent years I heard that one of them had come back and was helping out in our old parish. It was time to find out what had happened to one of the girls in black! So I met up with Sr Maureen and she told me her story.

At the idealistic age of sixteen, Maureen, from Cloncagh, County Limerick, was studying for her Inter Cert when she decided that her future was in the missionary field. She was one of a farming family of four girls and one boy. Growing up in a faith-filled home where the foreign missions were depicted as bringing God, hope and help to starving people, she wanted to carry the seeds of her faith and idealism to faraway places. She had just seen the film *Quo Vadis* and it had affected her deeply; *Quo Vadis* is a long saga depicting the persecution of the Christians in Roman times when they were thrown to the lions to be savaged for the entertainment of the Roman nobles. I can understand how this film at that time could have had such a dramatic effect. In that pre-TV era these films made a strong impact. They came across as reality. The idea of going out on the foreign missions to right all these wrongs appealed hugely to Maureen's sense of justice and equality. She dreamt of bringing peace and education to a troubled world.

It could have remained a pipedream, but Maureen was a determined young lady and so she sat down and wrote to many convents in pursuit of her ideal. To her amazement, they all wanted their recruits to bring a dowry into the convent with them. This was out of the question for her as money was not free-flowing in the rural Ireland of the fifties. She also wondered why you would need all this money if you were going out to do good on the missions.

Then fate intervened and she saw a write-up in a local newspaper about the profession of a local girl in Australia, and the address of St Joseph's Convent, Newmarket, was given. She promptly put a letter in the post to them. She had already discovered that they did not require a dowry. Accompanied by her parents, Maureen arrived for interview at St Joseph's; her family, like most in rural Ireland at the time, had no means of transport, so a local hackney car had had to be hired. All went well with the meeting and Maureen was instructed to finish her school year and come back in three months' time. After tea in the parlour they were given a tour of the convent, which was very impressive with its polished wooden floors and elegant curving staircase. She was furnished with a list of requirements and to this day she recalls vividly the huge efforts that her parents made to provide her with the very best. Having a nun in the family was regarded as a great blessing, and they got a loan from the local creamery to cover the expense. Her list included a dressing gown, and this was the first time Maureen had ever seen one. Another requirement was an umbrella, and they bought an elegant one that she could hang over her arm. But the most important purchase of all, as far as Maureen was concerned, was a beautiful pair of bedroom slippers, the first pair she had ever owned. She loved them.

Carrying a suitcase packed with a whole new wardrobe, each item tagged with her name, she arrived back at the convent. There she quickly fell into a routine of rising at half past five for morning prayer and Mass, to be followed by a day packed with study and regular prayer breaks. Every day the postulants walked up and down the long avenue with a study companion, learning off poetry and history. At the weekends there was a long walk to the Island Wood, which she enjoyed as it was good to get out into the freedom of the country and escape the confines of the convent. Sometimes in the evenings they gathered in the convent hall for Irish dancing.

But after six months Maureen was flooded by a huge wave of homesickness. She was filled with longing for home and ached with loneliness. She desperately wanted to see her mother and father, sisters and brother. She missed them dreadfully. Feeling trapped, she planned her escape. Getting away during the day would be impossible, so it would have to be at night under cover of darkness. Her plan was that she would slip out into the night and begin the long walk home. She could not carry too much with her, but her lovely bedroom slippers could not be left behind. But when the time came and she opened the door out into the black night, she lost her nerve. She was afraid to step out into the darkness. Her plan had to be abandoned. There was no choice but to stay put and cope as best she could with her desperate loneliness.

But soon to confront the young Maureen was a far greater trauma. A telegram came from home with the terrible news that her sister Nora had been diagnosed with leukaemia. She was just twenty. Her father came to collect Maureen, and the road home, for which she had longed so much, was now a traumatic journey to the Regional Hospital in Limerick. This was a newly opened, large impersonal hospital, where Nora already seemed to have slipped into a frightening sterile medical world. Her time was very short and during those weeks Maureen was allowed home each weekend to visit her. After the funeral she was allowed to remain at home for a few weeks to be with her parents. They were deeply appreciative of the nuns' kindness in allowing Maureen home for those few weeks with them. Had she decided not to return to the convent, it would probably simply have added to her parents' distress, as leaving the convent at the time was frowned on by society.

After returning to the convent, a numbed Maureen settled back into the routine, and six months later, with six other postulants, she was on her way to Australia. One can only imagine the suffering endured by the still-grieving teenager, not alone being separated from her bereaved family but also travelling to an unknown destination. At that time emigrants did not come home for many, many years and Maureen felt that she would never see her parents again.

The seven young girls boarded the train in Newmarket and travelled to Dublin where they were met by a priest who went with them by bus to Dun Laoghaire. From there they went by boat and train to Southampton. There they were joined by two nuns of the St Joseph's of the Apparition order and boarded a luxury liner. The *Iberia* was on its maiden voyage to Australia. This was a whole new bewildering experience for the young Irish girls who had previously never been out of rural Ireland. On board the liner they were delighted to meet up with a charming warm-hearted Capuchin priest, Fr Colga O'Riordan. He was young like themselves, and on his way to a challenging new world. During the voyage they became great friends with him and in later years he attended all the important occasions in their lives. It was the time of the Suez Canal crisis, so they travelled around the Cape of Good Hope. They disembarked in Cape Town and had a day touring the city, chaperoned by Fr O'Riordan. It was all new and exciting, and a long way from the convent in Newmarket. The adventure of it all helped to distract them temporarily from the heartbreak of leaving home.

The sea journey took six weeks. At night the young postulants went below deck and joined some of the stewards who were devout Catholics, to pray the rosary with them, and during the day they played games on deck. While most of the passengers suffered from seasickness, Maureen was blessed with steady sea legs.

Very early on the morning of 21 January 1958 they sailed into Sydney Harbour. Maureen, with her initial idea of going on the foreign missions still firmly planted in her mind, had expected to see black people on the shore! This was understandable because at that time everywhere in Ireland, on the counters of shops and pubs, were African Mission collection boxes topped with cherub-like black babies, and when you dropped in your money, the baby, by the power of some simple inward mechanism, nodded in thanks! It was a superb collection strategy, especially as children loved the nodding black babies, but it probably led to the belief that all foreign missions led to Africa. Maureen expected to see the black babies of the African mission boxes running around. But this was Australia, not Africa.

They were met by white Australian sisters and taken to the mother house in North Sydney. On arrival, there was a ritual of welcome during which they received the official uniform of the postulant, which was a full-length black dress and a dainty black veil to the shoulder. They were given their official name by which they were to be known from then on. It was the feast of St Agnes, so Maureen got the name Agnes, and also Ita, which was the name of a Limerick saint. So she became Sr Agnes Ita.

After some weeks Maureen was sent with two other sisters to a small remote community in New South Wales where the sisters of St Joseph had set up a school. Each day she helped out in the classroom. But after about six months the loneliness and isolation of this remote place got to her and a terrible homesickness set in. Still grieving for her sister and missing her family, she went through a hard time. However, while there she made one great discovery: she loved teaching. Realising that without the sisters these children would have no education at all, she knew that she now had the motivation to keep going.

Then followed two years in the novitiate. Prior to entering there was an assessment of each candidate. This gave the girls the opportunity to opt out and the congregation the opportunity to decide whether or not a girl was suitable for this vocation in life. Then began a period of fairly intensive study of theology and liturgy and a learning of the deeper ethos of the congregation. To Maureen's delight, the person in charge of the novices was Irish and this brought a sense of home a bit closer. She still missed home dreadfully. Life in the novitiate was very strict, with rigid rules, and all post was read. But because the forty-four girls there were young and light-hearted, they also made their own fun and entertainment.

At the end of two years there was another assessment and once again the girls were given an opportunity to opt out and the leadership of the order an opportunity to decide if the candidate was suitable or otherwise. At the time it seemed harsh if a girl was deemed unsuitable, but in the long run it was probably better than to find out later that it was the wrong choice. By then Maureen had no doubts about the step that she was about to take and knew instinctively that she had found her niche. She was accepted for profession and with forty others took vows for three years. As she recalls the day of her first profession, a glow of happy recollection washes over her. 'It was a glorious grace-filled day,' she smiled. 'I was filled with a flood of happiness and a sense of peace. I just knew that I was on the right road. But absence of family was a sadness on the day.'

She went to North Sydney Training College where she loved every minute of her training to be a teacher. Then she was missioned to the outback of New Zealand with two other Irish sisters. At the time, employment for many people in New Zealand was provided by a major undertaking of building huge dams to harness the rivers of this vast country for electricity. The people followed the work into remote places, resulting in many migrant parishes. The sisters travelled with the people out to these remote communities to bring education to the children. There was no other educational system.

But out in the bush the nuns had no source of income and depended totally on the generosity of the people for survival. 'We never went hungry,' Maureen said, 'and we learnt to cook everything that they brought us. Sometimes we were a bit perplexed by what arrived and when I saw my first pumpkin I was not too sure what to do with it.' She remembers the parishioners as being absolutely generous and wonderful. They were warm and welcoming and deeply appreciated the sacrifices that the nuns were making to bring education to their children. But Maureen did not regard it as a sacrifice. She loved teaching and was delighted to provide schooling to a whole generation who might otherwise have missed out. This was one of the reasons that she had become a nun. The fact that the lifestyle was primitive and lacking in luxury did not bother her at all.

Maureen was a natural teacher and loved her charges. Education was her field. Without the nuns many children would never have had the opportunity that education offered. As the schools of the order grew bigger and better, she moved up the ranks and became a headmistress.

She especially loved the Maori children who, she said, were as 'bright as buttons', though maybe not always academically. With their sense of story and music they brought the richness of their culture to the classroom and she, being Irish, felt a great affinity with their sense of family and tribe. They knew where they came from and who they were and had a huge loyalty to their own tribe. Their gathering place was called the 'Marae' and Maureen loved to see people dress up in colourful costumes for special occasions there.

As memories come flooding back Maureen remembered one lad in particular. He was a large young fellow who was a bit suspicious of the entire educational system and being taught by nuns did not impress him. He kept them at a distance, but Maureen did her best to engage with him. Then one day he arrived wielding a big strong stick and threatened Maureen that if she came too close to him she would get a good hard wallop of it! She was a bit scared of him, but tried from a distance to impart as much knowledge as she could. Years later she was very surprised to get a letter from him. He was in prison, which did not come as a huge surprise to her, but what did amaze her was that while in prison he had gone through a huge change and under the guidance of a prison chaplain, who was also a nun, he had become a born-again Christian. He wanted to thank Maureen for being instrumental in his conversion to a better way of life as it was she who had sown the seed of his conversion by her attitude: she had inspired him and helped him not to 'feel stupid'.

She remembered others too. One little girl was a brilliant student who soaked up knowledge like a dry sponge. 'She was a bundle of mischievous energy and was constantly in hot water.' Maureen smiled remembering. 'The teachers were forever trying to sort her out. In the play yard I used to say to her, "Next year you are coming into my class and then you will toe the line." My warning would always be received with a cheeky grin. Then one day I told her again, but before I could finish my ultimatum she cut in with an engaging smile, "And *you* will toe the line!" Maureen enjoyed her sense of independence and fun, especially at a time when you didn't answer back to someone in authority. She loved learning and flourished under Maureen's guidance, going on to third level where she graduated with the highest honours. She went on to play a significant role in the educational policy of the country. Without the nuns these educational doors would have remained closed to her.

Maureen became very close to some of her former students, in a way that was perhaps unusual for a nun of the time. She remembers one young woman in particular. 'Julie was a lovely girl, happily married to a great husband, with three lovely kids. When she moved away to another part of Australia I really missed her.' They kept in touch and one night Julie called to tell her that she was in great pain because she had fallen in love with the local priest. Every night for months they talked over the dilemma and gradually Julie's passion abated and eventually evaporated, and nobody but Maureen knew about the storm that could have wrecked her family. Maureen's common sense had won the day and Julie was forever afterwards grateful to her.

But whereas Maureen had found her true vocation, others were not so lucky, and she remembers one fully professed nun who wanted out simply because it was not the life for her. Getting out in those days was a long complicated procedure, not laced with the milk of human kindness, and after a long and protracted process of getting dispensation from vows, you walked out with very little and you just had to fend for yourself. Also, coming out of a convent was regarded almost as a disgrace, so you were not exactly received with open arms in the society outside the walls. But Maureen kept in touch with her friend and gave her all the moral support that she could and later encouraged her to make contact with the leader of the order, who gave her some financial recompense.

Over the years Maureen returned occasionally to Ireland but found the first visit home after eleven years challenging as her family had moved on. Her sisters were now married with young children. It was difficult to fit into this changed scene but subsequent visits became easier. The scene in New Zealand had also changed and now many schools were up and running efficiently and Maureen's management ability and teaching expertise led her into another field.

She applied for an advertised position in a diocesan education office and got it. A team of five religious was employed by the bishop to work in rural parishes who needed support. Maureen provided religious advice, administrative direction and guidance with liturgy. Once again, her people skills came to the fore and she moved from parish to parish, giving direction and help where it was needed. Her field of expertise widened and she got to know and became friends with a wide variety of people. She loved the New Zealand people, their openness and generosity.

Over the years, as Maureen grew older, going back after a visit home to Ireland became more difficult, so much so that eventually she decided that the ordeal of parting from loved ones back in Ireland was so traumatic it was best to stay in New Zealand. The order of St Joseph, in the meantime, had decided that the Irish nuns, if they so desired, were free to return home permanently. But Maureen was very happy in her adopted country and felt no desire to leave it for good.

Then the unexpected happened. The order had a chapter meeting of their sisters and hundreds of nuns from all over the world gathered. Maureen was nominated to thank the order publicly on behalf of the Irish sisters for the freedom to return home. Even though she was not one of those wishing to go, she had no problem speaking for those who did wish to return.

But when she got up to speak, an amazing thing happened: a huge unexpected emotional tide swept over her and she burst into uncontrollable tears. A wave of repressed longing had exploded inside her. It came totally out of the blue and Maureen was flabbergasted. It caused her to revisit her past. Had she kept a lid for years on the heartbreak of losing her young sister? And a lid on the trauma of leaving the family support system while still grieving? A lid on the loss of leaving her roots behind? The upshot of this deluge of suppressed emotions and the ensuing questions it raised caused Maureen to do a rethink. After careful consideration she decided that she too would go back to Ireland. The time to come home had arrived.

Back in Ireland her first job was the supervision of a small respite care centre in her home county. But when she retired from that, she felt that it would be the completion of a circle if a sister of St Joseph's were to come back to live and work in Newmarket where all the Irish-born sisters had begun their training. That parish now had just one priest instead of the three that had been there when she was a postulant. In Newmarket she became involved in the parish and particularly in its liturgical life – and wherever else there was a

HARBUTT'S
ckboard Ch
White

need. With her administrative skills and liturgical expertise, Maureen was a great blessing.

Her old convent has long since changed hands and is now the base for LEADER (Liaisons Entre Actions de Développement de l'Économie Rurale) projects under the guidance of Irish Rural Development. There are new houses on the long avenue leading up to what was once the convent, and Maureen has taken up residence in one of these. She is delighted to be involved with some of the activities of LEADER, whose enterprises greatly enrich the fabric of rural Ireland. The parish is enhanced and energised by Maureen's positive attitude and knowledgeable enthusiasm.

Recently, on the occasion of her Golden Jubilee, she returned to Australia and New Zealand, where she had spent so much of her life. She received the following acknowledgement: 'No gift could properly pay tribute to fifty years given in the service of God's people. Fifty years given so generously and with such joy and enthusiasm. Bless you, Maureen! You have touched the lives of so many and shown that this pilgrimage we are all on can be travelled with joyful anticipation.' All her life Maureen has adhered to the philosophy of her order's foundress Mary MacKillop: 'Never see a need without doing something about it.'

Chapter 10

The Other Side of the Mountains

Away in the distance across the valley from where I grew up were the Kerry mountains. They edged my childhood horizons and I often wondered what lay beyond them. Looking across at the changing colours, I sensed that the valleys beyond had to be beautiful. And when I grew up and visited them I discovered that they were indeed truly beautiful, but probably the most stunning of all was the Black Valley, which runs from Moll's Gap to the Gap of Dunloe outside Killarney. What was it like, I wondered, to grow up in that remote valley? To be a woman living in such a remote place? Years later when I met Eileen I found out what life

was like on the other side of my mountains.

Eileen was born and reared in the Black Valley. But when her mother Julia was born there in 1895 there was no question that she could remain. Beautiful scenery then did not provide a livelihood as tourism was not the industry that it is today. Emigration was the answer to their problem. One day when Julia was a teenager her mother suddenly said to her, 'Do you know, Julia, that you are going to America in the morning?' It was simply part of their way of life that the young went to England or America. So Julia went to the railway station in Kenmare and took the train to Cobh. There she boarded a liner for America and it took her six weeks to get to her destination.

She spent seven years in the United States, but the call of the beautiful Black Valley brought her back. In the final days of her visit home from America she met a friend in Kenmare who asked her, 'Why are you going back to America when the Black Valley is full of bachelors looking for wives?' 'There is only one man who would keep me from going back to America and that's your brother Denis,' Julia confessed. 'Let it with me,' her surprised friend told her. The result of that chance meeting was a wedding the following year when Julia married the love of her life and went on to rear a family of five, one boy and four girls, and Eileen, now eighty-five, is one of those girls.

When Eileen talks about growing up in the Black

Valley her face is suffused with a wave of delight. She had an enchanted childhood. She walked the three miles daily to the local Glen national school. The teacher at the time would live with a local family and as this did not always work out, or as the challenges of Black Valley living proved too much for young teachers accustomed to a different lifestyle, so teachers changed frequently and Eileen remembers five different teachers during her primary-school years.

After school Eileen often emptied her bag of books and headed off up the mountain with her siblings to pick wild strawberries, hazelnuts and blueberries. They picked until their bags were full and then sat on the mountainside and ate until they were full, and they brought home the rest. And in the valley below their house were two blueberry bushes on which they loved to feast.

During one winter hike up the mountains Eileen fell into a deep drain and hurt her hand. The local doctor could not travel due to the icy mountain roads and it was a week before her broken hand was set. But with a healthy diet and non-stop walking up and down the mountains the children were fit and healthy and able to withstand the challenges of Black Valley living.

Sometimes, if heavy rains came in winter, the water from the streams and waterfalls ran down the mountain and into their home – a disaster for her parents but very exciting for a child. And Eileen fondly remembers the music of the mountain streams in summer. Bord na Móna cut the turf and the valley women helped with the work of stooking it, and they were paid by the company. It was valuable extra cash. All the homes in the Black Valley faced the winter with a reek of black turf by the house and as Eileen's family lived in a forest there was no shortage of brambles and fallen trees for firewood too.

The family had seven cows, but farming in the valley was almost entirely sheep farming. The sheep grazed the mountains and sometimes her father extended his flock and rented more land from an elderly brother and sister who lived on the opposite mountain. Her father always watched the chimney of that house to make sure that smoke came out every morning – when it did, all was well, but if not her father went across the valley to check if they needed help.

Lambing time was hectic and often when a ewe had twins or maybe triplets, their father would give each child a pet lamb to feed with a bottle, and they always knew their own lamb no matter how many they had. They grew to love their pet lambs and when the lamb was sold and they got new clothes, that dress or coat never made up for the loss of their pet. Eileen's father had over three hundred sheep, but he would still notice if a particular one was missing and often came home at night saying something like, 'The one with the black face is missing', and he always searched until he found the missing one. The perilous mountain tops could be dangerous, even for the nimble-footed sheep. The newborn lambs announced the coming of summer and to this day Eileen loves the sight of a field full of sheep as they evoke a sense of peace and tranquility and wonderful memories.

As on farms all over Ireland, the pig was the main source of meat. Their pig was bought as a little *bonham* at Kenmare fair and fattened to feed the family. Eileen was never present for the pig killing because the baby pig had initially become her pet and she would try to warn it about the impending danger, advising it to run away. But the inevitable always happened and at an early age she had to reconcile herself to the tough reality of farming life. She remembers her mother washing the pig's guts in the running stream and turning them inside out and washing them again. They were then filled with oatmeal, onions and the pig's blood to make black puddings. The children took some to the neighbours, who would return the compliment when they killed their pig, just as we did where I lived far inland.

Every year shortly before Christmas a large car would suddenly arrive into the Black Valley. The coming of this impressive black car was a source of great wonder to the children and as soon as Christmas was on the horizon they began to anticipate its arrival and look towards Moll's Gap, waiting for it to turn into the valley. They were fascinated by the driver, who had a gold tooth, and by the two ladies who accompanied him. These ladies wore long luxurious fur coats which at the time were the ultimate stamp of wealth. They wore large fashionable hats and smelt of rich exotic perfume. When the car finally arrived it was surrounded by a flurry of excited children and the gentleman with the gold tooth and his two fur-coated companions doled out sweets, biscuits, dolls and a varied selection of toys. Some adults received gifts as well. The children christened the driver 'The Sweet Man'. Nobody knew who these people were and no money changed hands; it was a totally anonymous act of generosity. The people of the Black Valley recognised it as a Cork car and concluded that the man must be one of the wealthy merchant princes of Cork.

The week before Christmas, Eileen's parents would travel to Kenmare in the pony and cart. There the Christmas shopping took place and they came home with a big chestful of Christmas fare. This chest, which was lined with silver paper, had originally been a tea chest. On Christmas Eve, Eileen's mother would stuff the goose and that night they had a big supper, which always included a pot of jam, a luxury for the children. Behind the fire was a huge log known as Blockeen na Nollag that her father had brought in from the forest. This was put at the back of the fire and it smouldered away for weeks, making it easier to manage the fire over the Christmas period. One Christmas gift that Eileen remembers was a paper lantern that she loved playing with and that later served as a Christmas decoration.

Prior to the building of their own church in the Black Valley the people walked twelve miles every Sunday to Mass in Derrycuinnihy where *súgán* chairs provided the seating in the church. Having first milked the cows, they left home, fasting, at half past nine in the morning and returned at about half past two in the afternoon. If the river was in flood their father took each of the children on his back in turns across the swirling water. They wore wellingtons on the journey but carried their shoes for Mass. On arrival at the church the women and children went inside but the men stayed outside talking until the priest came. When the bell rang they too filed in.

In 1955 they built their own church, Naomh Muire an Choimín Dubh, in the valley, and this made Mass attendance a far less onerous undertaking. The church was built by voluntary labour, with donations from Black Valley people in America paying for the materials. Electricity came to the valley in the mid-seventies, which was twenty years after the rest of Ireland. In some ways this was almost a forgotten valley where a resourceful people depended for survival on their own abilities and on what the world around them provided.

When her mother was asked what time it was she would simply open the door and judging by where the sun was on the floor she could tell the exact time. Her mother loved music and dancing and constantly sang as she worked. Her favourite song was 'Maggie' – 'I wandered today to the hills, Maggie …'. At night when their father was gone across the valley visiting neighbours, her mother had them all out on the floor set-dancing.

At the age of fifteen Eileen went to Killarney to work in the Muckross Hotel, which is now the Muckross Park Hotel, where she worked for eight years and earned ten shillings a week. Every morning work began at seven o'clock when she took tea to the forty-two bedrooms. She worked with a light-hearted girl named Maureen, who was from Cork, and they often careered down the broad banisters from the top floor to make a swirling arrival into the lobby three floors below. Long before the luxury of en-suites, bedrooms were often removed from toilets, which could be at the far end of a long corridor. The solution was heavy earthenware chamber pots, some of which were colourfully decorated with roses. Eileen was averse to emptying these vessels of their contents so she made a bargain with Maureen that if she did the chamber pots Eileen would do all the rest of the work. So Maureen would proceed purposefully along the corridors bearing her cargo skilfully disguised beneath a draped towel.

When she got time off, Eileen took the bus home to Kenmare and walked the final stretch through the mountains, across the river and then up the mountain at the other side to her home. She remembers coming upon her mother cutting wild fuchsia on the mountainside and then the lovely smell of fresh bread that her mother had baked to welcome her home.

By then two of her sisters were already in London where she joined them to be a bridesmaid at one sister's wedding. She stayed for three months and worked in the cocktail bar of the Kensington Hotel. It was just after the war, when air-raid shelters were still a way of life, and she was taken aback by the smog and smoke of London. It was a big change from the fresh clean air of the Black Valley!

Then America beckoned and Eileen decided that she would go there and see this place where so many from the valley had travelled to make their fortune. At the time the procedure for getting to America was quite long and complex. To kick off the process she went to Dublin where she stayed with another sister and her husband. She had to go to the American Consul for a medical and then went to see an agent about booking her passage. She did not relish the prospect of a long boat journey so enquired about the cost of flying. It cost sixty pounds, which was quite prohibitive at the time, but to her amazement the agent informed her that she could fly for half-price if she facilitated the passage of a baby to a family in America. He told her that on the day of the flight he would pick her up, then collect the baby and take them both to Rineanna Airport (now Shannon International Airport). On the morning of the flight he picked Eileen up and they drove to a convent in Dublin and collected the baby, who was actually a little girl about three years old. Eileen had no idea why the little girl was travelling to America and the travel agent offered no explanation. The child clung to Eileen all the way on the long journey. Eileen never forgot her afterwards and often wondered how she fared. Due a terrible storm they had to come down in Finland, but Eileen has no recollection of being afraid. When they finally arrived in the US a family was waiting for the little girl – this was the fifth child they had got from Ireland. Eileen had no knowledge of the adoption process whereby American couples acquired Irish babies born outside marriage. It was years later when the full story emerged. This was just a little bit of the jigsaw when society, parents, the Church and the government colluded to brush these unfortunate mothers and children out of their hair. Years later when some of these children came back to find their birth mothers, the entire jigsaw fell into place.

Eileen travelled on to Chicago where she went for an interview and got a job in a restaurant. She loved the positive encouraging approach of the American people and spent twelve years there, regularly sending parcels back home. Often, as she wrapped up what in Ireland was known as 'the parcel from America', her tears mingled with the little luxuries that she knew would be so appreciated at home, and she felt that she was also posting back her tears to the Black Valley. She got great joy from sending home special items to

her mother, who had never indulged in buying herself luxuries, but Eileen remembered her admiration for special items of clothing in shop windows in Kenmare. Her mother had an appreciation of beautiful things and Eileen recalls going to a very exclusive store, Marshall Field's, one time to buy a real leather brown handbag with matching button boots. Their arrival in the Black Valley caused great excitement and the elegant boots fitted her mother perfectly. And when her parents built a new home she posted back all the curtains, to the great delight of her mother.

Then in 1963 she made a return journey home and still recalls the joy of being reunited with her mother off an early morning flight into Shannon Airport. When she came around the corner at Moll's Gap she saw afresh and appreciated more the beauty of her beloved Black Valley. On that visit home, Eileen married Michael in the Naomh Muire an Chuimín Dubh church, and he is still her lifelong companion. Michael had gone to America before her and come back after her. When the ceremony was over they went back to the family home for what was then called the 'wedding breakfast'. For days prior to the wedding the entire family had cooked and baked. After the breakfast people lined up around the kitchen floor and sets were danced to the music of local musicians. Later they were joined by the 'Biddy Boys', or 'straw boys', who were part of every marriage celebration. They all danced and celebrated into the early hours.

She and Michael returned to America for another four years and then came back for good in 1967 with their young son. Tourism had taken off in Ireland so they built a family home and guest house, which they still run together. To Eileen the Black Valley is the most beautiful place in the world and she looks back on her childhood there with the belief that it is very good to be stretched early in life and that it is possible to be happy on very little. There, as a child, she had listened to the call of the cuckoo and the musical tones of the cascade of water running down the mountains to the river. Nowadays, in early summer, she likes to return to her valley to hear the cuckoo and the music of the waterfalls.

Chapter 11

A Dependable Woman

In life we sometimes arrive at a place where our coping skills are stretched beyond their limits. When I was a young married woman with two small children, both my husband and I worked in the family business helping Uncle Jacky to run the village shop and post office where the postal delivery came in at six in the morning and there was an all-night telephone service, which meant that someone was on call day and night. Then the house next door came up for sale. I saw the For Sale sign on the gable end and wondered who our new neighbours would be. 'Aunty Kit', as she was known in the village, had run a guest house there for many years and had decided to retire. It never crossed my mind that *we* might buy it! Then one night on the phone to my

mother I mentioned that it was for sale and she straight away enquired, 'Are you not thinking of buying it?' 'Us? No, it never crossed our minds,' I told her in surprise. 'Well, think about it then,' she advised. 'Ye have no back entrance and that is no way to live on the side of the street.' This was the voice of a countrywoman who was used to wide open spaces and access to every corner of the farm. 'But we have no money,' I told her. 'Don't let that stop ye,' she advised. This was when bank managers demanded your skin for a loan and long before the Celtic Tiger was even a pup. My mother, on this occasion, was ahead of her time!

And so we bought this rambling old house in need of much renovation and finished up with a large guest house in the centre of the village. It entailed a few years of hard graft and a bank manager constantly breathing down our necks. In the middle of the second episode of building I developed a ferocious allergy in my hands, so much so that not alone did my hands look terrible but the itch almost drove me crazy, and I finally had to give in and go to our local doctor. He looked at them in dismay.

'Job for a skin specialist,' he told me unhesitatingly. And despite my protestation, that same evening I found myself across the desk from a frosty-faced consultant, who took one glance at my hands. They looked as if they had been buried for a week. Without even asking me, he announced, 'Into the Bon Secours this evening.' 'I can't,' I protested desperately. 'What do you mean you can't?' he demanded. 'I have small children and we are in the middle of a big building project,' I said, almost on the verge of tears. 'And I'm sure that you're a big help with that pair of hands,' he told me icily, looking at my hands as if they smelt as bad as they looked. 'But I need to be there,' I told him. 'Can you not prescribe something?' 'No,' he barked crossly, rising from his desk. 'Now, you are only wasting both my time and yours. So book in or go home.'

With no choice I found myself that evening ensconced in a four-bedded ward in the Bons. For two days I didn't talk to any of the other patients because I slept day and night and woke only when a nurse arrived with a bowl of black evil-looking liquid into which I immersed my hands. My snappy consultant came daily and sniffed disapprovingly by my bed. Finally I felt energetic enough to look around me and a friendly-faced woman in the bed opposite said, 'Whatever about those hands, what you needed more than anything else was a good sleep.' She was right and so was my frosty-faced consultant. I arrived home with much improved hands that I was afraid to use! Not much of a help in the prevailing situation of babies and builders.

Then one morning I met Maude on the street. Years previously she had moved with her elderly parents from a farm much further back in West Cork into a house just outside the village. She cared lovingly for both parents until they died, and then she upped and went to England to train as a nurse. Training with young school leavers cannot have been easy for her, but Maude was not one to flinch at a challenge and when she had completed her training she came back to her house and beautiful garden and took up a nursing career in a nearby hospital. Because she had a caring nature and great capability, she was a wonderful nurse.

Now she inspected my hands – they still looked like the paws of a skinned rabbit – and nodded, diagnosing a condition I had never heard of. She took a pen out of her bag and wrote down an unpronounceable name. 'That ointment will sort that out,' she told me. 'I have seen the condition before and this is the only cure.' She was right! After a few applications my hands were back in action. I was eternally grateful to her. But I never again took my hands for granted and on Maude's advice always wore gloves for tough jobs. She enquired regularly as to my progress and because of my hands we became friends. You could tell Maude your innermost thoughts and they never went further than her.

Then a mutual friend Molly became very ill and Maude and I sat beside her bed during her last hours while her husband paced the floor like a caged tiger. They had no children and no extended family. It was not an easy situation, but Maude took charge with inspirational sensitivity. She calmed the distraught husband and lovingly comforted the dying woman. She massaged Molly's hands and face and when the need arose delicately moistened her mouth. I knew no comforting prayers for the dying but Maude seemed to have an endless supply and a deep knowledge of exactly the right words to use when the need arose. As the night wore on I realised that Molly was in the hands of someone who knew her Kübler-Ross stages of dying. Maude had years of nursing experience during which she had been a comforting presence at many deaths and I felt that what I was witnessing then was a deep wisdom and love of humanity. I felt honoured.

When Molly finally peacefully closed her eyes in the early hours of the morning, Maude had travelled with her to the very edge of wherever it is we go when we leave this world. Maude's absolute belief that Molly was stepping into the arms of a loving creator filled that hospital room with a glow of hope, comfort and love. I realised then that my friend was an extraordinary woman.

A few years later Maude and I went to Lough Derg together. Now if you have never been to Lough Derg you cannot imagine a place more demanding of your physical and mental stamina. I have been there on a few occasions and if you were to ask me why, I would be hard put to explain my reasons. You arrive fasting since the previous midnight onto a cold miserable little island where you remove your shoes and walk barefoot over stony paths called 'beds', praying, and you starve for three days without sleep. Sounds crazy. It is! But for some reason beyond the logic of human understanding you leave that island physically and mentally refreshed and ready to meet any challenge that life decides to send your way. But while you are on the island you question the sanity of the thinking that brought you there. It is a place of total contradiction. One visit can be more effortless than you ever thought possible and you may well be cushioned into thinking that you have cracked it. But then you come back a few years later and that little island takes you between its teeth and pushes you again to the very edge of your endurance. You walk around in a stupor of sleep deprivation and starvation. The cold freezes you into the marrow of your bone or if the weather happens to be warm the midges eat you alive. There is no winning on Lough Derg.

But doing it with Maude was a whole new experience. To her it was a breeze. She climbed nimbly across the toe-battering rocky beds, lost in a meditative world of her own. The only source of sustenance available is dry toast and 'Lough Derg soup', which is boiled water with a shake of salt and pepper. This miserable meal is consumed once a day, and when Maude and I partook of it she savoured it as if it were a gourmet beverage. She endured the long night vigil of praying without sleep with stoic tenacity, helping others who found it simply too tough by taking them to the nursing bay where she sourced medical aid when the

'The best PRO
the dying ever had'
Guardian
Elisabeth
KÜBLER-ROSS
Living
with Death
and Dying
HUMAN HORIZONS SERIES

Chapter 12

A Family Secret

One day last summer I answered a knock on my front door and found two attractive young American girls standing there. 'We are on a rather strange mission and we think that you might be able to help us,' one of them told me. 'We have read your book *To School through the Fields* and feel that you understand how Irish life works.' I was more than a little bit intrigued by this statement and invited the two young women in. They introduced themselves as Suzanne and Rose. Suzanne proceeded to tell me a story that had begun to unfold at their father's funeral a few weeks previously. Her telling was so graphic that I felt I was there ...

As she watched her father's coffin disappear down into the grave Suzanne felt that the pain inside her would explode. The same pain as when her mother had been buried. It was back. Then she had been a young teenager with no idea of the dark days ahead, but now she knew. She and Rose had clung to each other during those terrible days after Mom's death. It was so good to have their father with them. Though shattered by his own loss, he still stood strong and helped them to cope. He had been the rock to which they had both clung. Slowly the pain became bearable and they recovered. Dad had been amazing and it had taken her a long time to appreciate the inner strength it had taken from him to be able to comfort them in the midst of what must have been his own terrible sorrow. And, of course, there were the three aunts – 'The Aunts' as she and Rose had always laughingly called them. Dad's three sisters.

Though these three aunts had left Ireland years before and had settled down and lived happily in America, they remained as Irish as if they had never left Kerry. The eldest of them, Aunt Susan, after whom Suzanne herself was called, was the matriarch of the family, and she doted on her two nieces. Unlike her sisters Mary and Nellie, she had never married and she loved the two girls as if they were her own children. Their mother had got on extremely well with her three sisters-in-law and included them in all family events. Their mother was an only child and having no immediate family of her own was delighted to be adopted by her husband's ready-made family.

After their mother's death Aunt Susan had moved in with them and this had helped them enormously. She was warm-hearted and comforting and saw them through their turbulent teenage years. Then Aunt Susan was diagnosed with terminal cancer. They were devastated, but she handled it with such faith and courage that they were strengthened by her serenity and bravery. The other two aunts rowed in and they all cared for Aunt Susan at home, where, they told me, she had died peacefully two years previously.

Suzanne was unprepared for the wave of desolation that now engulfed her father. She wondered if it was the delayed grief after their mom, now joined with this new tide of grief. It had submerged him. Mary and Nellie seemed to understand him better than Rose and herself and called constantly to the house, spending many hours chatting to him. But he had never recovered from the two deaths in such close succession, and his appetite for life was never again the same. His fatal heart attack, that had struck out of the blue, plunged them all into state of shock.

It was then that the girls learned about the family secret. Towards the end of the burial service, when the priest had finished the final prayers, Suzanne overheard Aunt Mary whispering: 'I wonder do they know?' 'I have no idea,' Aunt Nellie whispered back, 'he never said.' The exchange had an undercurrent of secrecy and urgency. Even in the midst of the funeral trauma she was taken aback. What on earth could they be talking about? Later, she told Rose about it. They were very puzzled and invited the aunts around to ask them about it.

The following evening the aunts arrived, Suzanne made tea and when they were all comfortably settled she decided it was the time to broach the subject of the graveyard conversation. 'Aunt Mary,' she began, 'in the graveyard yesterday I overheard you and Aunt Nellie wondering if we knew something and if Dad had told us. What was it?' She was not prepared for the sudden stunned look that flooded both aunts' faces. They looked totally shocked. Then their gazes locked as if looking to each other for guidance about what best to do. Slowly Aunt Nellie braced herself and took the initiative. 'Mary, tell them. It's time they knew.'

'Well,' Aunt Mary began hesitantly, 'this may come as a bit of a shock to you. We were never sure whether you knew or not ... Well, both of you always thought that Susan was your aunt and your father's sister, but that was not the case. She was, in fact, your father's mother and your grandmother.'

Her announcement was met with stunned silence. Susanne and Rose looked at their aunts as if they had taken leave of their senses. 'What?' they both breathed in shocked amazement.

Suzanne was the first to recover and very slowly, with an

emphasis on every word, demanded: 'You mean that we had our grandmother living right here with us and we never knew? What kind of goddamn carry-on was that?' Rose began to cry deep shuddering sobs. When Aunt Mary went to comfort her, Rose pushed her away. 'You wronged us. You robbed us. Why didn't you tell us? Now they're both dead and we can never talk about it with them. What the hell was wrong with you? We had the right to know.' Suddenly the enormity of releasing the long-hidden secret overcame both aunts and they too began to cry. Suzanne was the first to recover her composure. 'Tell us the whole story, Aunt Mary.'

Aunt Mary settled back into her chair, swallowed deeply and began to tell the story in a trembling voice. 'It was all such a long time ago. Susan was barely sixteen when she became pregnant. She was just a child herself really. We were all younger than her and hardly knew what was going on, but Susan disappeared for a few months. I found out later that my mother had sent her to stay with an aunt in Dublin where nobody knew her. When she came back a baby suddenly appeared in the house, and my mother told us that it was her own baby and we simply accepted it. It seems unbelievable now, but back then we were incredibly naive and totally ignorant of the facts of life. We loved the little fellow – your father – and he grew up with us and went to school with us. Some of the neighbours may have wondered about the whole thing, but there were no questions asked. At the time that kind of scenario was not so unusual. The alternative was that Susan would go into one of those dreadful mother and baby homes where they were treated very badly and their babies taken off them. In fairness to my mother she spared Susan that, and Peter had a good life with us. Susan, being the eldest, was the first to emigrate, and it was not easy for her. But our mother had a sister here in America and she looked after her, and then the rest of us followed on. We had no second-level education, not to mention third-level, but we knew how to work, and later we went to school at night and got on well. When all of us girls were here, Peter joined us and we sent him to college and he did well. Then he met your mother and had a great life with her.'

'Did he know that Aunt Susan was his mother?' Suzanne asked quietly. 'He did. As soon as Susan judged that he was old enough to know, she told him. And when you were born, I think he was very happy to call you after your grandmother.' 'Why did Dad and Aunt Susan never tell us?' Rose had calmed down as the story unfolded. 'I think that Susan never got over the trauma of the whole thing. Looking back now, Ireland in the thirties was a terrible harsh unforgiving place for young women. There was only one sin there then and that was to be an unmarried mother. It had a terrible shame attached to it. And I think Susan never got over the trauma of it all. I think she wanted to let things be once she had made her peace with Peter.' 'I wish we had known,' Rose said sadly. 'It feels as if we've missed out on a whole part of their lives that we could have shared.' 'We never told you because we felt that if Susan and your father wanted you to know they would have told you. It was their right to make that decision.'

'What about Dad's father. Who was he?' Susan asked. 'We were never quite sure and she never told us,' Aunt Mary said. 'She had gone to work on a neighbouring big farm and we thought that it might have been the son of the house.' 'I wish we had known,' Suzanne said sadly. 'I loved Aunt Susan, but it would have meant a lot to have known that she was actually my grandmother.' 'That man who was our grandfather cannot have been up to much,' Rose declared bitterly.

Having told their story, the girls looked at me hopefully for some guidance as to how to unlock their family secret. But this secret had long roots stretching back over many years. It could not be dug up overnight. It would take time and patience to get to the root of it and the girls had neither. They were flying back home the following day. They had checked school and church records with no success. My suggestion was to come back at a later date and spend time on the family farm and get to know the old neighbours. No doubt somebody back there knew. In Ireland there is always somebody who knows and the key is to discover who that is.

When they were gone I thought of all the hidden babies of Ireland now coming home, mostly from America, to find their roots. I wondered if the little girl whom Eileen had been asked to take to America ever came back. It is part of the human psyche to know who we are and where we come from. Our harsh society of that time did those babies and their mothers a huge injustice.

Chapter 13

The Salt of the Earth

The family plot just beyond ours in the local graveyard had always looked a little forlorn. It should not have been so because it was the grave of a man who, for the best part of his life, had been the local schoolteacher. He was remembered with great respect and fondness. But his grave did not reflect that. He had no children and there were no close relatives living locally, so there was nobody directly responsible for the grave. And though he had taught many in the parish, none of us felt it was our responsibility to look after it. It was probably a case of everyone's job being nobody's job, and that included me. The teacher had been a great gardener and when I first came to the parish he would bring me gifts of free-range eggs and a head of his first lettuce every Easter. But in this instance, I'm afraid, it was a case of eaten bread being soon forgotten.

Then, one day, the grave was transformed. It was totally cleaned up and had fresh flowers. It looked cared for and loved. As I stood admiring it, Ann, a local woman whom I knew well, came and stood beside me. 'Was it all right to do that, I wonder?' she asked. 'Would anybody mind, do you think?' 'Would anybody *mind*! Why the hell should they?' I answered incredulously. 'You never know,' she said nervously. 'But who did it?' I asked. 'We did it,' she told me, referring to herself and her husband. 'It seemed such a shame that after him teaching most of the parish his grave was not well looked after.' I came home feeling that a community that had people like Ann in it was not such a bad place after all.

She is one of those people who quietly makes the world a better place. Not talking about it, she just does it. One of a large family, she looked after her elderly mother, who was blind for many years. Her mother was lovingly cared for and died at home in her own bed, a rare blessing in today's world. Ann runs the family farm with the help of her two saintly brothers, whom she treats with loving kindness. Her husband, who runs his own business, is her staunch supporter and partakes in all her activities. Ann hides her light under a bushel, but, just like the neglected grave, when anything is suddenly done – quietly, without any fuss – one's thoughts immediately turn to her.

The only time that she was persuaded to step into the limelight was some years ago when it was decided that owing to the shrinking number of priests we needed to fill the gap with a morning prayer service, as our priest was overstretched with daily Mass in two churches. We once had two priests in the parish, but now like many other places we have just one. So, things had to change. It was decided to try to assemble six teams of two lay people in each to come in one morning in the week to do the service. Your team's turn would only come around once every six weeks, so it was not a huge commitment. It was a good idea, but who would do it? Not many, it seemed! Amongst a few others, Ann and her husband came to the rescue. She is always very reluctant to come forward in any circumstances but so few were willing she was prepared to go beyond her comfort zone.

Our church is cleaned by voluntary groups that we call the 'Clean Team', and we have six teams, so again your turn comes around every six weeks. Ann is on one of the Clean Teams, of course. And around the church is the graveyard. It is now like an extended garden. But it was not always so! At one time the side ditches were smothered in briars and so were the graves beside them. A group came weekly to attend to their own family plots and from that evolved the Graveyard Team. They began to come weekly to cut the grass and then eventually to attend to the entire graveyard. The team attends to any graves that are forgotten by families. Ann is one of the team who comes weekly to keep our graveyard a place of which we can all be proud.

Then the seats in the front of the church were a bit battered and neglected – until one morning they had a new, fresh look. You did not need to ask who had worked the transformation. Around some forgotten graves in the centre of the graveyard are fine old railings that had rusted over the years. Recently they donned a black glossy coat that will enhance them and extend their life. No need to ask who wielded the paintbrushes.

We hear a lot in today's world about how busy we all are with no time to spare for voluntary organisations. And yet it is often the busiest people who get involved. People like Ann keep kindness and caring flowing through the veins of our world.

To the Glory of God In memory of my Parents R.I.P.
Erected by Rev. P.A. Desmond P.P.

Chapter 14

The Island Woman

Like many other students of the 1950s I was introduced to Peig of the Blasket Islands when studying Irish. It created a deep curiosity about the isolation of island living and dependence on the whims of the sea. Island women had to stand alone while their menfolk were out wresting a living from the sea. Later, reading Patrick MacGill, I learnt about the potato picking in Scotland where the men from the west coast of Ireland had to go away to bring back hard-earned money. Islands like Achill were annually drained of their men and young people for months on end when they made the annual pilgrimage to Scotland. These island women had to rear the children and eke a living from the barren fields between the rocks while their husbands were away. I wondered what did this kind of life do to these island women. What was life like on islands like Achill? Then I did an interview about my book *Do You Remember?* on *The Tommy Marren Show* on Midwest Radio and the fallout from the interview finally put me on the road to Achill. 'A woman rang in very anxious to talk to you,' Sean, the interviewer told me. I thought this sounded interesting so I called the number he gave me. It was a woman called Nancy who told me that her mother was a great fan of mine and would love to talk to me. 'Her name is Ciss Flynn,' she told me and she gave me the number. I am of the age that if I do not do things straight away they could slip into a deep, impenetrable hole called 'Forgotten', and also I am a believer in the Lady Macbeth policy: 'If it were done when 'twere done, then 'twere well it were done quickly.' Well, sometimes anyway!

So I rang the number. A rich warm voice poured over me. 'Alice, *a grá*, I can't believe it! Aren't you great to ring. I am ninety-four years and have lived on Achill all my life.' 'You live on Achill Island?' I said delightedly. 'All my life, *a grá*,' she told me. 'Once ever I left to go to England but had to come back after five weeks because I missed the sea so much. I could not live without the sea. I have lived here all my life and seen many changes.' 'I have never been to Achill,' I told her.

'Ah, you must come to Achill,' she said. 'I grew up here one of eight. Every home in Achill then had about eight children.

We did not have much, but my mother was a great provider. She grew all kinds of vegetables and the sea fed us too. I love the sea. My mother had geese and sometimes when they went into the sea they swam way out. When she saw that they were gone out too far she would send our sheepdog, Happy, out after them in case they got caught in the strong currents and carried away. He would swim away out beyond them and turn them back, and swimming behind and around them guide them back in to shore where my mother would be waiting to house them for the night.'

I was fascinated. I came off the phone with the wonderful image of an Achill sheepdog swimming out to sea and shepherding the geese home. When I was a child on our farm, every morning and evening the sheepdog rounded up the cows to bring them home for milking. But I never knew that the unit of dog and master helped survival on the sea as well as on the land! By a strange coincidence I was already working on a book in which I was hoping to capture the essence of women like Ciss, women who have moulded the soul of Ireland. Now it was almost as if Ciss had walked onto the pages of the book. When I told her about it she said she'd love to be part of it. 'I am ninety-four years old,' she said. 'I want to tell my story before I die.'

It is about a five-hour drive from Cork to Achill, but it was a beautiful day as my son Gearóid and I drove up through lovely countryside. On a long drive an amiable travelling companion is a great plus as it shortens the road: the Gobán Saor knew what he was talking about! We planned to stay overnight on Achill and drive home the following day.

For some reason I had anticipated travelling over a long arched bridge into Achill but in reality the connecting bridge covers such a short span that you are almost unaware you have left the mainland and are on the island. But the mountains tell the story as they rise up around you like a reception committee. For the first time I fully appreciated Paul Henry's paintings and could see why artists are fascinated by the light of Achill. The mountains roll down to the sea and then rear back leaving craggy inlets, or *cluids* to use an Achill term.

There was little trace of Ciss's longevity in her lively stance and bubbly, warm personality. She was born in 1920, christened Kathleen, but this was soon changed to Ciss by her brothers. Here was a woman full of enthusiasm for life. After a welcoming cup of tea we went for a drive around Ciss's beloved island. We came to Slievemore, where she pointed out the deserted village, a row of little ruined stone cottages along the base of the mountain. 'During the famine the people left those little houses and moved down to the sea that could feed them.' There was something incredibly sad about the rows of abandoned, roofless ruins that told the story of a terrible period in Irish history.

Then an elegantly designed small stone church graced the mountainside and Ciss's daughter Nancy took up the story.

'That Protestant church was part of the Achill Mission set up by the Revd Edward Nangle. He came to Achill on a charity mission when the island was in deep trouble. English Protestants gave him money to help the islanders and he leased land from the landlord, Sir Richard O'Donnell, at the swampy lower slopes of Slievemore. He built the "Colony", and in it was a church, a hospital, a kitchen, a printing press, an orphanage, post office, dispensary, corn mill and farm buildings, all surrounded by fields reclaimed from the wet mountain slopes. There were two substantial dwellings for two clergymen, a steward's house and thirty cottages. They fed the people during the Great Famine in the 1840s but only if they converted to their religion. This created a terrible dilemma for the starving population and started a bitter religious conflict that divided the people. Those who converted and got fed were known locally as the "Soupers".'

Then we passed a well-kept graveyard and Ciss said quietly, 'That's the fire graveyard. Ten young lads from here who were potato picking in Scotland in 1937 died in a big fire when the shed where they were sleeping went on fire. The shed was locked on the outside by the employers and they couldn't get out when the fire started. Their bodies were brought back to Achill. Even after all these years I can still remember the heart-breaking scene of ten coffins being carried on the shoulders of the island men across the bridge from the station to the church.'

Then we reached Ciss's present home, which was built in 1932 by her father, who was a stonemason, and her brothers with the help of a government grant of one hundred pounds. Nestled further along from that house and facing out to sea was the roofless stone ruin of the house where she, the youngest of the family, was born in 1920. Part of the gable end and one tiny room remain. Long soft grass grew inside. As we stood looking in the door of what was left of her childhood home, Ciss told the story of what had been. It is interesting that in many cases when a new house was built the old ruin was left beside it to tell the story of what went before.

'We had two small bedrooms, one for the boys and one for the girls and one big room. Now, the big room was the kitchen and in the corner nearest the fire was the *caileach*, which was the place for my parents' bed. It was surrounded by rich drapes and these came from Scotland or were bought at the fair that was held on the last Friday of every month on the island. On either side of the fire were two butter boxes, with lids, and each box had a cushion on top, covered with different crocheted patterns of wool. These were comfortable seats and one box contained clean socks and the other socks to be washed. Our table was about six foot long with a bench on either side – a 'form' as they were called – and a chair at each end. The dresser had pride of place in our kitchen, with sets of china, plates of all shapes and sizes, and jugs, all of which came from Scotland. On the shelves my mother had floral shelf-paper with scalloped edges. For special times of the year she dressed the shelves with lace, handmade by her niece Maggie Joyce, who taught lace-making and needlework on the island. Maggie had learned these skills from the nuns in Galway.

'My mother baked brown and white soda bread and the flour for this was bought by the hundredweight. The bread and sugar were stored in the bottom of the dresser and the tea in tin tea caddies on the mantelpiece over the fire. Twice a week she made a churn of butter, sterilising the churn beforehand by washing it out with boiling water, replacing it with cold and then dropping a limestone she had reddened in the fire into the churn, replacing the dash and top and allowing it to fizz up to sterilise it. There was a chest inside the door for storing the milk and butter, and this was sterilised in the same way.

'Our houses then were built with stones bound together with lime plaster and this was got from the limestone that was burned in the kilns, the remains of which are still around the island. In my grandparents' time if you happened to gather some fine large stones for your building the landlord's agent could come and take them off you for their own use, and if they needed workers you were supposed to drop what you were doing and go with them. For your day's work you got a meal of salted herrings and buttermilk.'

'I'm surprised to hear that there was a landlord on Achill,' I interjected.

'Oh yes indeed,' she said, shaking her head. 'Once they tried to evict my grandparents, Sally Rua and John McTigue, from this little house. The agent had wanted my grandfather, who was also a stonemason, to drop what he was doing and go with them to do a job, but my grandmother, who was called Sally Rua on account of her red hair, would not allow him go, so the landlord put on a rent which he knew they could not pay. Then the landlord's agent threatened to evict them. But when news of the eviction got out, the island people gathered, with the priests, who stood with them. They came from all over the island and brought every container that they had, filled with cow's urine, and each time that the agents charged the door they were showered with buckets of it. Now, the law at the time was that an eviction had to take place before three o'clock, and if it had not taken place by that time it had to be abandoned. Luckily it was high tide and some of the neighbours wrestled the crowbar off the agent and threw it as far out into the tide as they could, and as the deadline passed they prevented the agent from knocking off the cornerstone and so saved the house. This was a fairly regular occurrence for people who were courageous enough to stand up to the injustices and bullying of the landlords and their agents. Another thing that could happen at the time was that if you had a good cow it could be taken off you by the landlord. You had no redress because the landlord was the law.'

'Did the islanders always stick together?' I asked.

'Oh they often had fierce rows,' Ciss said, smiling, 'but even if they had a falling out and were not talking to each other they still came together for the *meitheal* to pick the potatoes and cut the turf. The turf took a lot of work, from cutting to footing to drawing it home with the donkey and creel.'

'And how long had your father's family lived here?' I asked.

'For generations,' she said. 'As I said, my father was a stonemason, using mostly dry stone and even now, after more than one hundred years, examples of his work, including houses and bridges, can be seen in many parts of the island. He loved to fish, mostly from a rock known as Conal's Rock, and what he caught he gutted and cleaned before bringing it home, and if he caught a lot he shared it with the neighbours. He recited the rosary every night in Irish and each of us said our decade – and it could be a lengthy exercise as he had a lot of trimmings and often prayed for neighbours and their problems and even for the animals. As a youngster I could not understand why the animals had to be included in our prayers, not realising the vital part they played in our lives. When his children began to go out at night he always said the rosary before we went. He died suddenly in 1931 aged sixty-six, and in those days on the island the coffins were made in the house of the deceased by a local man who was good at carpentry, and after being waked for two nights the coffin was brought by horse and cart or tied to the roof of a car and brought directly from the house to the graveyard.'

'And your mother's people,' I asked, 'were they here for generations as well?'

'No, my mother was a stranger,' Ciss said. 'She was Nancy Nan Gallagher from across the bay.' Ciss pointed across the water. 'But that's just across the water!' I protested. 'Didn't matter, she was not from the island and for that reason she would be considered a stranger.'

'And how did she fit in?' I queried. 'She never tried to,' Ciss said. 'She always held herself a little distant from them because that was the way she was. But as the years went by they realised what a great woman she was and began to treat her with the height of respect. She grew carrots, turnips, parsnips, onions and all kinds of vegetables, and she grew two kinds of potatoes – Kerr's Pinks for the table and Arran Banners for the animals. She boiled the Arran Banners and mixed them with seaweed and fed it to the pigs.' Ciss pointed to a field behind the house, further away from the sea. 'That was where we grew the vegetables and potatoes and when we were planting the potatoes we used the animal manure and over it we put a bed of seaweed and placed the seed potato on it. The seaweed was great to grow everything. We cut it off the rocks, which was freezing cold work and very hard on the hands – and there were no rubber gloves then.

We drew it up to the house in the donkey creel.'

As Ciss talked we climbed down the little grassy slope from the ruin onto the stony seafront that was strewn with seaweed. The sea was practically at the front door.

'When we lived here the sea was further back,' Ciss explained, 'but since then it has eaten into the land. We call this the *cluid*.' She pointed to a sheltered inlet and then along the beach, remembering where the different animals were housed, and I realised that we were standing in the centre of what had once been their farmyard.

'We had a donkey, four cows, two pigs, a flock of about twelve geese and a lot of hens. And when we took out the hot ashes from the fire we put them under the perches in the henhouse to keep them warm. Our animals were very close to us and my mother kept everything spotlessly clean, which was not easy with no water in the house and no electricity.

'We had a pig for selling and a pig for the house. When they were young a ring was put in their noses to prevent them from rooting up the garden. The night before the pig for selling went to the fair he was well washed. At the fair he was sold to the highest bidder. A replacement was bought as a *bonham* the following spring. When the other pig was killed a piece of fresh pork was given to the neighbours and the remainder was salted for six days in a wooden tub of coarse salt and then taken out and hung from the rafters, which were not very high. All the neighbours who had a pig did the same thing, but no two pigs were killed at the same time so there was fresh pork available for a longer time. As children we loved the pigs, who became our pets, and they loved nothing better than to lie down for somebody to scratch their belly. Fish were also salted for when food was scarce. The goose feathers and down were used to fill the ticks and pillows for our beds and, of course, the sheep fleece was wonderful.'

Then Ciss stooped down and picked up what to me looked like green lichen that was growing off the rock. The spongy little plant was a soft delicate shade of green. 'This is what my mother used to dye the sheep's wool and she also used the yellow whin, onion skins and different pieces of tree bark for a mixture of colours. But first the sheep's fleece was washed and rewashed in a big timber tub, and because the seawater did not suit the wool, that meant drawing fresh water to the tubs. We children danced on the wool until it was snow white and then my mother raked and combed the fleece and teased it into threads. She knit socks and jumpers and used the loom to weave materials of different colours. When she was spinning she would have her own dyed wool in various colours beside her and she would add in little bits of different colours as she spun, making her own flecked thread.'

Then Ciss turned and looked out to sea, before continuing, 'My father loved music and was always whistling a tune. As soon as he could afford it, he bought fiddles with the potato-picking money and taught my brothers how to play. Strange thing was that he could not play himself, but he could whistle any tune perfectly and gradually the lads picked it up. The fiddles were hung along the wall over the hearth to keep them safe and dry. On fine evenings they practised on their fiddles sitting outside the house. When they were playing for a little while the seals near the shore began to make a whistling sound, calling to the others further out, and then they would all swim in right up to the edge of the water listening to the music, and when the boys stopped playing they swam away.'

She pointed to a headland that curved inwards at the edge of the bay. 'Out there is the Gob, and that was where the Scottish boat docked when they came to pick up the potato pickers, or the "tattie hokers" as we called them. All the young boys and girls on the island went tattie hoking. Some of them were very young – children really – when they went. The currachs took them out to the big boat. They left early in the year and came back before Christmas with the money they had earned. It was hard. But that was the way it was. In Scotland they worked long hours and slept in big sheds called "bothies", the girls at one end and the lads at the other, with a division in between. It was in one of those sheds that the fire happened in '37 when the ten young lads from the island died. One of the stoves took fire and the bosses had locked the shed on the outside and the lads couldn't get out.' Listening to Ciss you could still feel the sadness that accompanied all those partings and the terrible memories of the fire.

'Sometimes when the currachs went out to the big boat some of the locals who were not going to Scotland went out to have a look at the boat. Then they came back in when the currach returned for more passengers. When all the workers were finally on board the steamer made its way down the channel. The families left behind would follow along the headland, waving their loved ones goodbye, until the steamer was gone from view. I remember well the black and red funnels belching out smoke and steam and the lonely sound of the horn as it passed through the narrow channel and then disappeared from view.' As we left the headland I felt that the history of a whole tribe was woven into that *cluid*.

Later that evening back at the house, we sat around the table and Ciss talked about other island customs. 'Many of the weddings were the result of matchmaking and in some cases the bride and groom met for the first time in the church. Sometimes the bride and groom would travel together to and from the church in a car, but it was mostly bicycles, and there was always a competition to see who would be first home from the church as the winner would get two big mugs of porter – everyone else got one in the first round of drinks. Wedding presents were unheard of then. There would be a dance in the wedding house, with tea and bread and jam in a neighbour's house. Jam was a big treat in the war years unless you made your own. The dance went on all night or until the porter ran out. There was only one man on the island who could tap a barrel of porter properly and he was invited to every wedding. Music was by local musicians and that time there were people in every house who could sing or play the fiddle or melodeon.

'Back then it was a terrible shame for a girl to have a baby outside of marriage and that shame was felt by the whole family. I remember once when it happened the priest "read" the poor girl from the altar, which was very upsetting for the family.'

'What happened to the girls? Did they go into mother and baby homes to have their babies?' I asked.

'Not usually. The girls stayed at home with the family though they seldom came out during the nine months and usually the family or a sister reared the child. In Achill we looked after our own.'

Then Ciss began the story of her own family. 'There were eight of us in all, five boys and three girls. I was the youngest and the boy before me died at the age of two and it took my mother a long time to get over that. Our two eldest brothers went first to Scotland and then to England and in time got jobs for the other brothers and brought them over. In those years almost all the husbands worked overseas and came home for Christmas. Then they stayed to set the crops and cut the turf and when that was done they went away again to work.'

'You never emigrated?' I asked Ciss.

'Once, but only for a very short time because I found that I couldn't live without the sea on my doorstep. And as well as that, someone had to stay with my mother. At that time there was a preparatory exam for a scholarship to a teacher-training college. The teacher felt that I could pass this exam and asked me to do it, and when I refused he visited my parents to put pressure on me, but I still refused. I felt that I would not pass it. Maybe if I was not the only one doing it I might have given in, but to do the exam I would have had to go to Achill Sound, which was seven and a half miles away. I would have had to walk or cycle and I thought that it was too far. I did not tell the teacher or my parents that all I really wanted to do was to learn to dance! They were all mad with me. The day following my refusal my eldest brother, Tom, started to make a small creel with sally rods and when I was foolish enough to ask him what it was for I was told, "This is what you'll have on your back for the rest of your life." No further questions asked!

'The same Tom was the most stubborn man that God ever made. He married an island girl and before the wedding my mother told her so. They went to England and on the next visit home she was pregnant and decided that she wanted to stay at home with her mother and have her baby on Achill. But Tom was against that and told her that if she stayed he would not send one penny home to her, and that was exactly what happened. But he continued to send the usual money home to my mother and every week my mother went across the island and gave the money to his wife. My other three brothers, Michael, Martin and Con, never married and every Christmas came home from England. They were so good to us. They brought clothes and shoes and anything we wanted. After the war we could not get tea on account of the rationing and they would smuggle it home in the tubes of their bicycles.

'It was wonderful when everyone came home for Christmas, and we were all so happy to be together again. But when the time came to go back a gloom descended on the island. Husbands, fathers, sons, uncles and often daughters and sisters too were going away. A big van came to pick them all up and take them to the boat. At that time there was practically no traffic so we heard the van almost as soon as it came on the island – the sound of its engine travelled all over the place. Eventually it came to the bottom of our hill. We listened as it stopped at the first house and then at the different houses up along. Slowly it came nearer and nearer, and then we knew we were next.

'My sisters Sarah and Maggie went to Scotland potato picking and then later to England, like all the other girls on the island. Maggie was fourth in the family and she came back and married a man from Belmullet, where they lived. They had seven children and when the youngest was a baby Maggie was diagnosed with terminal cancer, with a very short time to live. She was thirty-eight. Sarah and I went to Belmullet, which was a long way away then as there were no cars. Maggie didn't know that she was dying and her husband asked me to tell her. It was the hardest thing that I ever had to do. But I somehow got it said the best way that I could and assured her that we would look after the children. I asked her did she want to come back to Achill to be buried. She said that she would stay in Belmullet to be near the children because no matter where they went they would probably eventually come back to Belmullet. She died that night. The day after the funeral a nurse in the hospital gave me a little brown purse. In it was one pound note, one shilling and her wedding ring.

'Three of the children came to me, two went to Sarah and two stayed with the granny in Belmullet, who was a pure saint of a woman. She had thought that she could manage them all, but because she was up in years that was not possible. The youngest, who was only sixteen months, could not settle away from his granny, so he went back to her. Little Mary, who was only three, would often help me lay the table and remind me that "This was the way Mammy did it." I found that so sad. It was the worse period of my whole life.

My heart bled for the children and I lost weight and my hair fell out. A local tonic was stout heated by a hot tongs – I drank it once but hated it so much that I couldn't take it again. But gradually I recovered, and being near the sea helped. There is healing in the sea, sitting beside it and listening to it. It healed me. I kept the little brown purse safely on top of the press in the kitchen and one day when one of her boys was a teenager he came across it and stopped dead in his tracks. 'That's Mammy's,' he said slowly and I wondered what memories it ploughed up in his mind. 'Would you like to have it?' I asked, and he nodded. And when Mary was getting married I gave her her mother's wedding ring.'

'You must have had a great husband,' I said.

'The best,' she smiled. 'He was the kindest of men and a great husband. Both of my children were born at home, and when Nancy was born my sister Sarah came home from England to be with me. Because she had emigrated when she was very young, Sarah had missed out on a lot of what my mother had told me. So when Nancy was born with a caul over her face Sarah was very upset because she had never heard of it. She was shocked when she saw this sheer veil with scalloped edges covering the baby's face and head. The veil was so delicate that she could see the baby's face clearly through it. She thought how terrible if the child has to go through life wearing this veil! But the doctor knew what it was and gently lifted it up and slipped it over the baby's head, much to Sarah's relief. The neighbours all came to look in on the child, and when Máire Mhór, an old islander who had delivered many babies in her time, saw the baby her words were, "*Bhuel, ní raibh fearg ar on Athair shiorraí nuair a chum Sé í seo*" (Well, the Good Lord wasn't vexed when He created this little one). The lucky caul is very rare and occurs only once in 180,000 births. The story goes too that captains of ships would pay good money to have one on board because it is believed that any ship with a lucky caul on board would never sink.'

Ciss had told me her story with no embellishments and absolute honesty. She had had a hard life, but it had not made her hard; instead it had woven a warm woman full of textured memories. This woman, who had struggled, cried, laughed and loved here on the island, had not only survived all that life had thrown at her but is a goldmine of rich remembrances and the much-treasured heart of her family.

That night a violent storm raged around Achill and as the wind pounded the windows I wondered what it must have been like years ago living in that little stone house facing out to sea with no heating, no double glazing, no insulation and the wild Atlantic belting in on top of them.

Chapter 15

Behind Closed Doors

An awareness of the existence of the Poor Clare nuns came into my life at an early age. When I was six, my younger brother Connie, aged four, died in the Bon Secours hospital in Cork. The hospital was next door to the Poor Clare monastery on College Road. My mother must have made contact at the time with the Poor Clares because an awareness of their existence, and also the sense that they were a source of comfort to her, filtered through to me. Later, when I spent a week having my tonsils removed at the age of twelve in the same Bons, the children's ward overlooked the monastery of the Poor Clares. Through the open window we could hear their bell tolling regularly calling them to prayer. I wondered what was going on behind those closed doors.

At the time my father had a young nephew in the Franciscans, Brother Matthew, who arrived every summer to our farm wearing a flowing brown habit and strapped sandals, and doled out holy pictures, scapulars and medals. He was happy and cheerful, and I had a vague idea that there was some connection between the Franciscans and the Poor Clares. Over the years I became aware that many people wrote to the Poor Clares in times of stress and anguish in their lives. This led me to the belief that when you were in financial straits you went to the bank, when you were in dodgy health territory you went to the doctor, but when you were in dire straits in any other department you called in the Poor Clares. They were the God bank! Their praying presence seemed to bring untold comfort to all who made contact with them. Once when a critical friend of mine demanded, 'What are those women doing locked up praying when they could be out in the world doing some good?' I lost the cool. 'Don't you think that there are enough of us out in the world and when you look around at the world, we're not doing such a great job, are we?' I had become a defender of the Poor Clares.

The Poor Clare Order, inspired by St Francis, was founded by St Clare of Assisi in 1212. It was a monastic order of enclosed contemplative life with sisters taking vows of chastity, poverty, obedience and enclosure. Their vow of enclosure is the one that perplexes most people. The order spread around the world and came to Cork in 1912 when a local merchant prince, Walter Dwyer, decided to build a monastery for them on College Road. His motivation was not entirely without self-interest as his favourite daughter had entered a Poor Clare monastery in Belgium and he wanted to have her near him. He had the money to build the monastery, but he would need the bishop's permission to bring in the order as well as Poor Clare sisters who would be willing to help set up the foundation in Cork. He turned for help to an old and trusted friend of his, a Jesuit priest, Fr Willie Doyle. Fr Willie approached the Carlow Poor Clare abbess, who gladly sent a band of five sisters. After a lengthy process the bishop's permission was granted and the way forward was cleared for Dwyer's dream to come true – and so the building began on College Road. Ultimately his beloved daughter returned to Cork and the official opening of the Poor Clare monastery in Cork was celebrated with Midnight Mass on Christmas Eve 1914. Down through the years they have become a font of comfort and prayer to the people of Cork and further afield.

To me they were a source of puzzlement and wonder. How did they survive and stay sane behind those walls and closed doors? I knew very little about them but I had come to the conclusion that there must be something going on in the lives of these women that was beyond my limited understanding. Or was it beyond all understanding? I was very curious.

Then I heard that a niece of Brother Matthew had joined the Poor Clares. This girl was no starry-eyed teenager with romantic illusions but a working girl out in the world, enjoying the good life. She had grown up on the family farm in the midst of a large family. In the usual Irish way her family and ours crossed paths at weddings and funerals, but apart from Brother Matthew, who was a bit of a one-off, we would never have considered them as very religious. In our house it was my mother who was the one who brought religion to the fore because the Taylors generally took a slightly less dedicated view of religious activities. One would think that we were not exactly a potential sprouting ground for a Poor Clare. So a Poor Clare in the family came as a big surprise. But also as a source of puzzlement. How was this going to work out? Was it a flash in the pan? Would she stick the pace? But stick the pace she did, and seventeen years after her profession she is the one to whom all requests for divine help and prayers are still directed when any trauma hits the family. Recently, when a younger member of our extended family underwent chemotherapy, she was encouraged and supported by her cousin in the Poor Clares and found that the letters of support and comfort sustained her through her ordeal.

With the decision to write this book came the time to meet up and find out about our Poor Clare. I wrote to College Road with my request and it was arranged that one afternoon I would visit her there.

I stepped into the little courtyard in front of their chapel and knocked on the door of the small lodge. The door was swept open by a pleasant-looking woman with a warm welcoming smile on her face, and she told me that Sr Anthony Mary was expecting me. This lovely outgoing secretary was obviously the order's link with the outside world. She led me along a short corridor past a little walled garden where there was a statue of St Francis and into a bright airy room. At one end of the room was a low timber partition, about waist-high, and from there up to the ceiling ran some very open wrought ironwork in the shape of a dove holding an olive branch, a symbol of peace; it was quite decorative and not in the least bit suggestive of a barrier. I had thought that I would be peering in through iron bars!

At my side of the railings was a comfortable chair and table, and on the inside of the partition was another chair. My appointment was for half past two and on the dot Sr Anthony Mary floated in, wearing flowing brown robes, with her smiling face encircled in a gleaming white headpiece. I knew from family data that this woman had to be in her early forties, but I was looking into the clear-skinned face and sparkling eyes of a teenager. She exuded tranquility and delight.

After a warm handshake she freely answered my questions and told me, 'The call to religious life came as quite a surprise to me and at seventeen the last thing that I wanted to do with my life was to be a nun! I attended school at the Mercy Convent in Mallow and during my final Leaving Cert year one of the young Mercy nuns talked to us about her vocation, and it was then that I felt the first divine prompting in my heart. Had I known Jesus at that time I think I would not have found it such a fearful prospect. I did my best to forget it and decided that it was not the life for me. My three older sisters were working at the time and one of them was preparing to get married. My friends too were all excited about the future, so the path to religious life seemed a lonely one to me and a bit different. I thought that I would be missing out on so much that I wanted from life and hoped that some day I would get married and have children.

'So I tried to find my niche in the world and did a secretarial course and got a job. I loved sport and adored stylish clothes and sometimes shocked my mother by what I spent on an outfit. Once, after buying a lovely new jacket, I was driving Brother Matthew back to Cork after a visit home and my mother was in the back seat. He was bit of a rogue and said, "Eileen, that's a beautiful jacket. How much did that set you back?" He knew well that my mother had her ear cocked in the back seat. So I fobbed him off and as we got out of the car in Cork he grinned at me and said, "You were too smart to tell me what you spent on that jacket with your mother listening." "I knew what you were up to," I told him.

'Despite the fact that I was enjoying life I felt a certain

emptiness and the inspiration to give myself to Jesus as a religious was always there at the back of my mind. Indeed, after my father died, the call became stronger. I always feel that those who are gone before us are not far from us.

'Then one evening I popped into St Mary's church in Mallow and sat quietly there, pondering over my life. I thought that there had to be more to life and felt that I was only living on the surface. I realised too I could not move on with my life unless I faced the fact that I could have a religious vocation. Was that what was missing in my life? So there and then, in the twinkling of an eye, I surrendered my life to God. I can't quite explain what happened, but life has never been the same since. At that moment a tremendous joy and peace entered my heart and with it an inner strength and conviction about my faith. It's as if a light had been turned on. I understood there and then that my life was part of a much bigger plan, which stretched right into eternity. My outlook on life changed and a whole new horizon seemed to open up before me. The fears I had of following Jesus disappeared. My faith, which had been dormant for years, was reawakened in that moment of surrender and I sensed new life bubbling up within me. I didn't really know what would happen next. I trusted that everything would work out fine. I had discovered the meaning and purpose of my life in the blink of an eye.

'As I was leaving the church I visited a little side altar of our Lady of Perpetual Help and entrusted myself to her. I returned to work in the family business and later that day found an old picture of our Lady of Perpetual Help hidden away in a dark corner of a shelf. I felt that she was telling me that she would always be there to help me. The picture is now hanging beside my bed. That day changed my life and many of my friends noticed the change and remarked on it. I felt happy and confident with my decision.

I contacted Fr John Bosco, a Franciscan priest who was a friend of the family and also spiritual assistant to the Poor Clares. He arranged for me to visit the Poor Clares in Cork. I remember feeling very nervous, almost terrified, as I stood outside the monastery door, but when I met one of the sisters I immediately felt at peace as if I had come home. After a few visits it was decided that I would do a "live-in"' for two weeks to see how I would feel about it. My "live-in" began on the 14th of June, which was the anniversary of the death of Brother Matthew, and ended on the 27th, the feast of Our Lady of Perpetual Help. Most of my family thought that I was going through a phase that would soon pass, a bit like a bad 'flu from which I would eventually recover. My mother was very accepting of my vocation, but the Poor Clares, she felt, were a step too far.

'I was given a great hunger for the Lord and went to daily Mass and regular confession and wanted to spend more and more time with the Lord in prayer. The Angelus, which I had forgotten, was one of the first prayers that I was inspired to pray again, and the rosary too was beginning to take a central place in my relationship with the Lord. My old lifestyle no longer held any attraction for me.

'Then I received a visa for the United States and to further test myself I headed off to Boston. My mother bought me a one-way ticket! I think she was hoping that the bright lights of America would side track me from the Poor Clares as she was finding it difficult to deal with their life of enclosure. My best friend was working in Boston and I lived there for a year, sharing a house by the sea with her and other girls. I got a job taking care of a lady with Alzheimer's, which was a great blessing, and on my day off I helped out in a homeless shelter run by the Franciscans. Down the street from where we lived was a little adoration chapel and in there I continued to pray for the light of guidance of the Holy Spirit. The thought of the religious life never left me and I began to realise that the life I was living was never going to be enough for me. Gradually I accepted that only the Lord alone could satisfy me and that it was His will that I enter the Poor Clares. There are lots of things that I could have done with my life, but the Lord only wanted one thing. He has a plan for everyone. So I returned home and told my mother and family. My friends were more than surprised by my decision.

'I entered on the 8th of September 1994, the Feast of the

Birth of Our Lady, and received my Franciscan habit and the name Sr Anthony Mary of the Holy Family. Six years later, during the Great Jubilee year of the Incarnation, I offered my life to God in solemn vows of chastity, poverty, obedience and enclosure. The journey continues and God is full of surprises.'

As Sr Anthony Mary told her story with honest simplicity I felt that I had journeyed with her into the monastery. But having arrived there I now wanted to find out how the Poor Clares spent their day. She was more than happy to tell me.

'The day is divided between prayer and work. It begins with a "little knock" on our cell door at half past five in the morning to which we reply, "God reward you." The sisters assemble in choir (the monastic term for chapel) and at six o'clock we pray the Angelus and offer our day to God through the Morning Offering Prayer. We have daily exposition of the Blessed Sacrament from six in the morning to eight in the evening. The people can also share in this great privilege of Eucharistic adoration from seven in the morning to six in the evening in our public chapel. Throughout the day there is always a sister in prayer with Jesus while the Blessed Sacrament is exposed. Our entire day is centred on Jesus, who is truly present in the Blessed Sacrament. During those early hours of the morning we settle down to our first meditation of the day, which leads into Morning Prayer, a part of the Divine Office. The Divine Office is the Church's official prayer and is composed of hymns, psalms, scripture readings, readings from the Fathers of the Church, intercessions and the great universal prayer, the "Our Father". Six times during the day, and once at midnight, we come together to chant the Divine Office on behalf of the whole people of God. It's a prayer of praise, worship, intercession and thanksgiving to God. Indeed, every possible human need finds an expression in this great prayer.

'At half past seven in the morning, Monday to Friday, we attend Mass, the high point of the day, when we renew our self-offering to God, in union with Jesus. At weekends Mass is at ten. In the public chapel just to the left side of the altar a glass partition with an embossed chalice and host can be seen. This is opened before Mass, which enables us to join with the people in our public chapel for the celebration of Mass. After Mass we spend time in thanksgiving and then we have our breakfast.

'After breakfast each sister has some time to attend to her duties – preparing the vegetables, cooking, sacristy work, sewing, gardening, letter writing, answering the doorbell, cleaning and other household duties. Our work is simple so that we do not extinguish the spirit of prayer and devotion but aim to be occupied with God alone in the silence of our hearts.

'The next part of the morning is given to spiritual reading, a very important part of our daily spiritual nourishment.

Each sister is free to choose a book. The Word of God is the most important word that we can read, or the life of a saint – anything that will help foster our relationship with the Lord. At a quarter to ten we gather in choir to pray *Terce*, the first of the three "Little Hours" from the Divine Office.

'We are open to receive the public every day (except Monday and the first Sunday of every month) from half past ten to half past eleven in the mornings. Many people avail of the opportunity to call and ask for our prayers. The intentions are many and varied, and all find an echo in our hearts as we come before the Lord to pray.

'At twelve noon we pray the Angelus together, followed by our second "Little Hour", which is called *Sext* (Divine Office). Then it's time for dinner and afterwards we do the washing-up together. At half past one we pray for the dead, including our benefactors, those who die tragically all over the world and all those recommended to our prayers. This is followed by our final "Little Hour" which is called *None*.

'From two to four in the afternoon our parlour is again open to callers. During Lent, November and December, and when we are on retreat, we are not open to visitors. During these times we try to create a little extra space for the Lord – a space in the heart where each one is called to communicate with God. Each sister has her own time of Eucharistic adoration during the day, a time to worship God and be renewed by His loving presence, and also bring to Him the needs of our brothers and sisters throughout the world. During the day each sister will make time to pray "The Way of the Cross", a traditional Franciscan/Poor Clare devotion. In the afternoon, we also have time for further study to deepen our understanding of our faith and Franciscan/Poor Clare charism. This time can also be used to develop a talent, for example playing a musical instrument.

'At half past four we have our second meditation time of the day, followed by Evening Prayer, and then the public can join us for the rosary at half past five. On Sunday evenings at five o'clock we have Rosary, Evening Prayer and Benediction with the public, and to our delight many people join us. At six it is time for the Angelus, followed by supper and recreation. Recreation is our time of relaxation and we share some prayer requests received during the day, exchange family news and enjoy a chat at the end of the day.

'Throughout the day the monastery bell is rung, calling us to prayer, and our final bell of the day is at half past seven, bringing us once more together around Jesus in the Blessed Sacrament to pray Night Prayer and the Divine Office. We retire at about eight o'clock.

'We rise at twelve midnight to pray *Matins* (Divine Office) and have some quiet time for meditation, returning to bed at a quarter to one. During that time we hold in our hearts all those who work through the night – parents caring for newborn or sick children who may have to rise from their beds more than once during the night, young people out socialising, our emigrants, anyone in any kind of distress and, of course, the dying and those who watch with them. Our prayers reach out beyond the four walls to places and people where we cannot physically go ourselves. On entering and leaving our choir, we pray the prayer which has come down to us for over eight hundred years from St Francis:

'We adore you O most holy Lord Jesus Christ,
Here and in all the churches throughout the world
And we bless you because by your holy cross
You have redeemed the world.'

As Sr Anthony Mary described the unfolding of their day she drew back a curtain and revealed a world that was very far removed from the world outside their walls. And yet, by their quiet prayerful presence, I felt that they are enabling many to cope with that world. In a recent survey done in America, it was discovered that violence decreased in a particular area where a number of people meditated, even though the violent and the meditators had no visible connection. During our time together in the quiet parlour, we had covered Sr Anthony Mary's journey into the monastery and a day in the life of the Poor Clares, but now I was about to tread on very sensitive personal ground.

Her younger sister, Patricia, had recently died of cancer

next door in the Bon Secours hospital and Sr Anthony Mary had spent some time with her. Patricia had a young family and had left behind a broken-hearted husband and grieving mother. It was also very difficult for Sr Anthony Mary and her family to lose their younger and much-loved sister. At the mention of Patricia's death Sr Anthony Mary nodded her head slowly and said gently, 'Even though the Lord had prepared me for Trish's death I still hoped that she might be healed. I had all our monasteries praying for her. She would be such a loss to John and the children and she was so close to my mother. But God had a different plan and even though we don't fully understand it now, we trust that things will work out. There is a lawn separating our monastery from the Bons, so I was able to slip across quietly each day to spend some time with her in her final weeks.

'The evening that she died, John had gone home to milk the cows; there had been no sign of change in her condition all that day. Trish passed away quite peacefully, shortly before John came back. It was hard for him, but our destined time is fixed by God alone. God's ways are not our ways, as we were to find out. As the night rolled on, my family began to go home, but John stayed on and after some time my cousin Bernie and I joined him. As John began to reminisce about his life with Trish, the strangest thing happened: Trish's face seemed to light up and a beautiful radiant smile spread across it. In fact, the more John talked about her and of their time together the more radiant the smile became. John noticed it, and leaning over her he said in a surprised tone, "Oh, she's smiling!" Eventually John too went home while Bernie and I stayed behind to pray. As we were leaving, Trish's beautiful smile had faded. It was as if her spirit had waited for John to come back and she wanted to share with him the comfort of saying goodbye.'

As I left the Poor Clare monastery that evening I felt very privileged that I had got a glimpse into what goes on behind their closed doors. These women are an invisible link between the human and divine, and while they may appear to be far removed from what is happening in the world outside they have their finger on the pulse of what is going on. They hear two news headlines weekly and read a newspaper on Tuesday, which is probably quite sufficient. But their greatest source of contact with our world is the people who bring every conceivable problem in their door, looking for help. The Poor Clares are a contributory factor in keeping our world a more bearable and saner place for many in trouble. They are truly inspirational women.